T0078075

More to Life

*A Skeptic's Journey from Depression to
Spiritual Awakening*

BRITT SEVITT

BALBOA.PRESS
A DIVISION OF HAY HOUSE

Balboa Press books may be ordered through booksellers or by contacting:

Balboa Press
A Division of Hay House
1663 Liberty Drive
Bloomington, IN 47403
www.balboapress.com
844-682-1282

The author of this book does not dispense medical advice or prescribe the use of any technique as a form of treatment for physical, emotional, or medical problems without the advice of a physician, either directly or indirectly. The intent of the author is only to offer information of a general nature to help you in your quest for emotional and spiritual well-being. In the event you use any of the information in this book for yourself, which is your constitutional right, the author and the publisher assume no responsibility for your actions.

Print information available on the last page.

ISBN: 978-1-9822-5770-5 (sc)
ISBN: 978-1-9822-5771-2 (e)

Balboa Press rev. date: 12/16/2020

To My Beautiful Children,

I hope and pray that you will hear the calling of your souls and always follow your hearts - not your heads, nor the herd, nor what you think others want from you.

Be true to yourselves. No one else. Being true to yourself is being true to God. Each soul is a spark of the Divine. Find your true self and you have found God - the Godliness in each of us. Everyone here is unique and on a different journey. Follow yours.

Contents

PART 3: ANALYSIS & INSIGHTS

PART 4: HINDSIGHTS & FORESIGHTS

Acknowledgements

Benjamin, for your unwavering patience, kindness, acceptance, love and support. I always joked that God didn't need to challenge you, that instead he sent you me. And boy, have I challenged you! Forgive me. I could not have got through this without you. I am truly grateful that you have accompanied me on this rollercoaster journey called life. I love you. Always have, always will.

Sean, Mili & Liam, I hope you can forgive me for the mother I was. I always did the best I could with where I was at the time. I adore you guys. You have taught me way more than I have taught you. You are my teachers and my inspiration. Thank you. Sean, for showing me determination, persistence, values, motivation, discipline, and dedication to creating a better world. Mili, for teaching me patience, kindness, joy, acceptance, gratitude, and living in the present moment. Liam, for demonstrating to me authenticity, compassion, oneness, passion, intuition, and honesty.

Mum & Dad, for always loving me, caring, and wanting the best for me. For bringing me up in the best way you knew and with what you had. I am truly grateful for everything you have done for me. I hope you can forgive me for the times when I didn't honour you as you would have liked.

My Siblings, for being you and for embracing this middle child with your love.

My Friends, past and present, old and new, for being there, for loving and accepting me even when I disappeared off the radar, retreated or hibernated for weeks, months, years. For being there for me when I couldn't be there for myself, when I couldn't even bear you to be there for me and for when I wasn't able to be there for you.

Michele, Nicki, Liora and Baruch, for all being integral parts of my healing. You each played important roles in helping me escape my prison and reach peace.

Elisheva, Benjamin, Debbie, Jamie & Sarah, my editors & proofreaders, thank you so much for all your hard work, time, support, patience, and dedication.

To the Divine, for helping me find You. For giving me this opportunity to grow and for helping me connect to my true self, my soul, my God spark. For all the challenges and wonderful blessings in my life. For guiding me through this incredibly difficult but beautiful journey called life.

PART 1

BACKGROUND

The Story Begins

*"There is no greater agony than bearing
an untold story inside you."*
- Zora Neale Hurston

T hank you for choosing to read my story. Writing a book was never one of my plans or desires for this lifetime. However, in 2018 my life turned 180 degrees overnight with a sudden spiritual awakening, and I felt a strong urge to write a book, at the very least to explain to my children what had happened to me. Years of clinical depression and anxiety disappeared during this unbelievable and supernatural event. My world changed overnight, and I underwent radical changes. My cynicism and skepticism for anything spiritual or alternative was challenged as I began to see the world through very different eyes. I continued to write, documenting, and reviewing my newfound spiritual understandings along with my insights, hindsights and foresights. This book is the result.

I have had to fight through much fear and resistance to publishing this book, knowing that many will think I'm weird or crazy. However, I believe that everything I have experienced is part of my soul's path, and that includes the need to share my story. This book comprises my own personal experiences, insights, and opinions. It is *my* truth. Please take what resonates and leave the rest.

A little background...

I always felt different growing up, like an outsider looking in. I felt detached from my body, I can barely explain it. I was a thinker, always up in my head. I had a conventionally happy childhood with parents who loved and cared for me. Somehow though, I became hypersensitive to criticism, despite knowing that with the same parenting, my siblings did not feel criticised and did not develop the same low self-esteem. I found it difficult to be myself. In fact, I'm not sure I knew who that was.

Brought up in a modern orthodox Jewish home, Judaism and religious observance were significant parts of my life. However, I didn't feel a true connection to the Divine. I kept the laws and traditions out of belief in God and fear of him too.

Studying was difficult for me. As a young child, I was often reprimanded for being fidgety and not concentrating. Not fulfilling my potential was a recurring theme throughout my education. I pushed through with undiagnosed ADHD and memory difficulties. With hard work, I received a Bachelor's degree in Psychology and Philosophy. I then went on to complete a Master of Philosophy at Cambridge University.

One would think being in such a prestigious University would bolster my self-esteem, however it had the opposite effect. I felt like a fraud and an impostor. Attention difficulties meant that I struggled with reading and I mastered the art of only skimming summaries or abstracts of books and research papers. I made excellent grades without reading a single research paper from start to finish. I felt like I had faked and dodged the system and even the renowned Cambridge University had not found me out.

Clinical depression and anxiety set in during my twenties and the next almost two decades were spent trying medications and talk-therapies to try to relieve my suffering. Throughout these years of mental illness, I took every medicine offered. I was diagnosed as treatment-resistant. I suffered through many different drugs and their side effects. One by one, they were found to be ineffective, I was taken off them, suffered withdrawal and put on something else. Even after all those failed attempts using modern medicine, I still preferred that over anything 'alternative'. I was a true skeptic about anything remotely holistic, alternative, or spiritual.

As far as I was concerned, alternative, holistic, and spiritual practices were a load of nonsense. All of them. If hard-core, scientific, psychiatric drugs could not help me then no way would flowers, plants, vitamins or waving hands work. So, I did not try any of them.

As you read this book, you will see that my own empirical evidence led me to shed my skepticism. From speaking to others I have met on this journey, I realise that my old standpoint was at the extreme end of the skeptical spectrum. I was dismissive, arrogant, and simply couldn't accept anything I couldn't understand. As you will find out, eventually I had no choice and began to embrace the 'woo'.

Wearing a Mask

"To be yourself in a world that is constantly trying to make you something else is the greatest accomplishment."
- Ralph Waldo Emerson

Most of my life I had been wearing a mask. That is, playing a role that was not the real me, but a version of myself that I believed I should or ought to be. The person that I thought my parents, family, friends, and teachers wanted me to be.

The mask slipped on in early childhood as family, religious and societal conditioning told me what to want and how to be. Subtle, gentle pressures tell us what to believe and how to act, to the extent that I honestly had no idea what the real me wanted or who she was. Being so detached from my true heart and desires, my life felt like a lie.

Wearing a mask and living inauthentically was severely damaging. I didn't know how to access my true self and lacked the courage to live that way even if I did. I clearly was not living in alignment with my authentic self and the consequence was deep unhappiness.

As the years went by, I realised I wasn't the only one who wore a mask. We all do to some extent. It is rare to find a person who says it *as it is* and our social-media-obsessed culture only exacerbates the issue. Doesn't everyone seem to have a picture-perfect life on Facebook and Instagram?

After the birth of my first-born son, I was acutely aware of the mask I 'needed' to wear. I was struggling with depression, and my new reality was as a mother to a newborn with very little control over my life. I was surrounded by friends and family beaming with delight for us. Don't get me wrong; I was over the moon with my gorgeous baby boy, but I was dealing with such difficult emotions that I felt I had no choice but to suppress them. Maybe no one else has such a hard time? Perhaps everyone else can manage fine and it was just me who couldn't cope? And so began many years of a thicker mask and my inability to tell people what was really going on inside.

This depression wasn't fleeting, nor just postpartum. It was a depression that lasted for many years.

A few years ago, a friend lent me "Carry on Warrior" by Glennon Doyle Melton. In this book, the author describes trying to make her insides and outsides match. It was evident to me that mine did not match. I'm a compulsive truth-teller and cannot lie. I suddenly realised my whole life was a lie. Having insides and outsides that didn't match felt like the ultimate dishonesty to me. Being pathologically honest but not true to myself didn't sit well at all, as you can well imagine.

A Holocaust educational trip to Poland, where I visited the concentration camps empowered me to begin slowly unpeeling my mask. Standing at the doors of the gas chambers of Auschwitz, I faced the stark realisation that life was too short not to be our true selves. There, I found myself making a promise to make my insides and outsides match. I decided to start being my true, authentic self and to tell people the truth about me. My experiences in Poland compelled me to open up to people I had only just met and release some of my most private thoughts. It felt good to be open and honest. To peel off a layer of the facade. To stop the act. To stop being a different person on the inside and the outside.

Whilst determined to continue this journey, I was still depressed and anxious inside, though my acting skills were exemplary. Those who didn't know, wouldn't know. It was well hidden by a chirpy persona that went out and put on a happy 'normal' face. I was ready to match my insides and outsides, but I didn't know whether that meant bringing my insides out, or my outside in! Bringing my depressive self to the exterior didn't seem like the best answer and I had no idea how to begin to feel happy on the inside.

I realised the only way to get my insides and outsides to match was to let people in. The more I let people into my crazy tortured mind, the less crazy and tortured it seemed. I hoped that the more I felt accepted by others, the more I would be able to accept and love myself. I learned that the key to having matching insides and outsides is to combine the two and be accepting of the whole package.

I returned from Poland empowered with the resolution that I was going to let my insides out. I began to write down what I considered my crazy thoughts, theories, and stories. However, I never had the guts to do anything with what I wrote and to further open up. The empowered feeling I had brought back with me from Poland withered away. In fact, for a long time I did exactly the opposite, I shut people out. The tougher I found life, the more I would push people away, hibernate, retreat, and play small. I felt so guilty being depressed because, objectively, my life was blessed. I wasn't suffering with many of the things others in this world deal with, like famine, poverty or illness. I didn't feel I was worthy of friends or a support system. I didn't expect people to spend time with a self-obsessed, miserable, moaning person who couldn't appreciate how good she had it. So, I retreated. At the time, I barely realised how much I pushed people away. I was so caught up in my own world, just trying to get through each day, unable to breathe, unable to be there for anyone, least of all, myself.

A year later I began to unmask when I took to Facebook and 'came out' about my years of suffering with depression. My mask was off, yet the months and years that followed were even harder. I often regretted that post. I retreated even further from Facebook and from people. It hadn't made it easier and I wondered why I had crazily, spontaneously, out of the blue written that post. My mask was off, and it felt naked and raw.

It became clear to me then that I had several masks, not just the one hiding my depression from the world. All my other masks were still firmly on. The masks of what I should be like, how I should act, what I should be doing etc. Layers and layers of conditioning and influence prevented me from connecting to my true, authentic self.

Treatment-Resistant Depression

"Never give in to defeat or despair. Never stop journeying
merely because the way is long and hard. It always is."
- Rabbi Lord Jonathan Sacks

I lived in a highly stressed, anxious state. A state in which decision-making was almost impossible. I lost all sense of perspective and panicked at the thought of making the wrong decision or not dealing with an issue adequately. One seemingly small item would become the focus of my anxiety for years and my life consisted of flipping from one issue to the next. Before each depressive episode, my anxiety would reach a peak. I would become aware that I was being irrational and disproportionate, but even knowing that, or being told it, didn't help. I was out of control.

The peculiar thing is that I was barely even aware of the extent of my anxiety disorder. I thought depression was my real issue. I knew certain situations stressed me out and that I was highly strung. I also knew that before slumps of major depression I would get irrationally anxious. It is only in retrospect that I can see how anxious I was all the time, and how much the anxiety as well as the depression impacted my everyday life.

How can I try to explain what depression feels like?
For me it was waking up in the morning not having any

good reason to get out of bed. Any reason could be used as an excuse to beat myself up. I told myself I was an awful mum, awful wife, awful daughter, awful employee, and my family were better off without me ruining their lives. I felt useless. Everyone was actually better off without me. No one could say anything to make me feel better. Inside my sick head, everything anyone tried to say to make me feel good was twisted into an insult.

I could prove how loathsome I was. Try telling me otherwise and I would give a million answers that proved just how awful and hideous I really was. Try complimenting me and it was like insulting me. It just gave me another reason to twist the compliment in my head, proving how it wasn't true and how the giver did not really know a thing about me. I knew the truth. I was useless and hopeless. I couldn't do anything right. I ruined everything and everyone's lives around me.

The worst of it was that somewhere deep down, I knew I was lucky and blessed. So I beat myself up even more. I had a great husband, great kids, great home and great life. How dare I be like this? I believed that everyone around me wondered why I could not just pull myself together and look at all the wonderful blessings in my life. And I thought it too.

It didn't end there. Depression totally affected my physical day to day life as well. My body became lethargic, achy, and lacking energy. It felt like everything stopped functioning. I had difficulty doing even basic things. Getting dressed, showering, cooking, the laundry. It was all so utterly overwhelming.

I went out and saw people, but behind the mask, my mind was in torment. It was pained, low, drained, heavy, aching, sad, lonely, misunderstood and trapped.

Just the question 'How are you?' would set off my internal self-defeating dialogue and I would beat myself up. Because even if I replied with a simple 'Fine,' my mind was racing with the truth. I was not fine, but I should have been fine. My only motivation to get better was for my family. Because they deserved better.

I didn't want to do anything to get better. Everything I did was such a massive effort for me. I felt like no one realised the strength it took to try and get better for those I cared about. Basic things like getting out of bed, leaving the house, seeing people, going to a shop, making a phone call, therapy, doctors, cooking, and exercise were each a major emotional and physical feat. Every minute I was not in bed, ideally asleep, was a huge unappreciated effort that wasn't paying off. I wasn't feeling better being out of bed. I was feeling worse. Because it meant being awake with my tortured mind.

There were periods when I was so depressed for so long that I would startle myself when I felt a smile on my face. It felt weird to smile or even laugh. I had lost my ability to do either naturally.

My depression lasted over seventeen years. It varied from dysthymia - an ongoing constant form of mild depression, to several bouts of major depression. My official diagnosis was 'treatment-resistant' depression. Over those years I saw over sixteen psychiatrists and psychologists and tried thirty different psychiatric medications.

I totally identified with people who committed suicide. The pain and anguish that comes with living inside a pained mind. Even if not actually suicidal, I was never afraid of it all ending and often wanted it to. Living was the scary bit. The possibility of years and years ahead with my tortured thoughts is what scared me the most.

And then, I hit an all-time low and wrote the following:

"In the words of Eckhart Tolle 'I can't live with myself any longer'. I swing between the unawareness that my irrational and deluded anxiety and depression aren't real and the full awareness that the way I am being is abnormal."

My husband dragged me to a new, emergency-appointment psychiatrist. As we sat opposite her she asked me whether I thought about dying. I told her that I would never consider suicide. I couldn't leave my family with the stigma and guilt of me killing myself. Despite my very real depression, I was always aware that even in my darkest days when I believed everyone was better off without me, that the stigma of my suicide would destroy them. I told the psychiatrist that, although suicide is not an option, if someone were to offer me a quick way out - like getting a serious illness or dying of natural causes - I would take it in a shot.

I was sobbing when I said this. I buried my head in my husband's lap and could barely finish my sentence. My rationality reappeared and I realised how awful what I was saying really was. I wanted to feel normal, whatever that was, and yet I just couldn't.

I hated myself even more than I did before. Because what sort of ungrateful, selfish person who has everything she needs in the world dares to think like that, let alone say the words out loud?

Low Self-Esteem Goes Hand in Hand with Depression

"The man who does not value himself,
cannot value anything or anyone."
- Ayn Rand

I t became clear to me through my years of depression that self-esteem is critical for pretty much everything in life, especially happiness, fulfillment, and growth.

On the outside I looked put-together, happy and living a perfect life, but my inner reality was very different. I would joke that I had a degree from Cambridge University, but what use was it when I didn't have the self-esteem to sit in a job interview?

Social media can be a disaster for those with low self-esteem. Thirty seconds on Facebook or Instagram is enough to make us berate ourselves and remind us of how useless we are compared to others. Simply by looking at other's photos of their awesome achievements, exemplary culinary skills, perfect parenting, beautiful beach bodies and idyllic holidays, these posts can trigger an inner dialogue of shame. Frankly, social media should come with a warning label of how much it can damage your self-esteem. And on top of that, it isn't a true representation of people's lives. I've often called Facebook, Fakebook. A fake picture of what people's lives are like. We mainly only get to see those perfect pictures and moments, not the ones where they look like crap and the kids are having tantrums and meltdowns. Most people are wearing a mask too and we only see the bits of their lives they want us to see.

Depression helped me realise that physical appearance, money, or success are not what bring you happiness or self-esteem. It doesn't matter how blessed you are or how many wonderful things you have in your life. Depression and low self-esteem do not care if you are tall, short, fat, thin, ugly, successful, rich, poor, or famous.

I would sigh to myself when I would hear conversations where people would imply that if only they were thinner, richer or more successful, they would be happy. I wanted to shake them and tell them that being rich or skinny isn't going to make them happy. Happiness is not based on any of these things. Look at all the rich, gorgeous, successful famous people who suffer from depression or addiction! It was clear to me that happiness needs to come from within. Not from something external, material, or physical. We often think we can achieve happiness by external means, but these are often distractions, coping mechanisms and addictions. True happiness will never be achieved from the outside.

Low self-esteem is rife nowadays. People simply are not loving themselves as they should. Emotional wellbeing is at an all-time low. Anxiety and depression are at an all-time high. The stereotype of a depressed person in bed crying just isn't accurate. There are many fully functioning people around the world who suffer from depression.

Low self-esteem is a risk factor for depression and we never truly know what someone else is going through. Many people were shocked when I 'came out' about my depression. They were so taken in by my mask they genuinely had no idea how miserable I was. We need to stop judging, stop comparing, stop assuming. We are all wearing masks covering up our inner world. That gorgeous, perfect, organised, intelligent, fun, successful person we are making assumptions about may well be living in a tortured mind. Their mask covers up their inner world. It could be anyone. Our best friend, our doctor, our cousin, our teacher. We may never know. The only thing one can do is be a little bit kinder and more understanding to everyone and especially ourselves. To not compare ourselves nor try to be like anyone else. To just *be* ourselves. The solution is loving ourselves.

An Adult Woman with ADHD

"Everything in life serves as a challenge and test to elevate us. Therefore it is right to be grateful for the opportunity to learn and grow through tackling this real life experience."
- Moshe Chaim Luzzatto

I n my mid-thirties, I (incorrectly) thought I found a possible reason for my suffering. Although I had studied Psychology, I didn't know a thing about ADHD. The sum total of my knowledge on the matter was the image of a hyperactive five-year-old boy bouncing off the walls.

I had a major depressive episode and found myself attending an emergency appointment with a visiting psychologist from the United States. At the end of our session she casually mentioned that she thought that I might have ADHD. How utterly weird, I thought. An adult woman with ADHD?! Does that exist? In my mind ADHD was just for little boys.

I went home and googled 'Adult ADHD' and filled out an online quiz. Reading through the questions one by one, it gradually dawned on me that they described me perfectly. Suddenly so much about my life to date became clear. It offered an explanation for my education struggles, fidgeting, inability to concentrate, impulsivity, hyperactive thoughts, bad memory and tendency to hyperfocus. ADHD seemed to explain so much about me, my personality, education, childhood - my entire life in fact. It offered a possible reason for not fulfilling my academic potential, my low self-esteem and constant feeling of being misunderstood.

I mistakenly got excited thinking I had unearthed the root cause of my depression and assumed that a different range of psychiatric medications would magically take all my pain away.

While the pieces of the puzzle were falling into place, it was bittersweet observing the havoc this condition had wreaked upon my life. Nevertheless, there was a degree of comfort in having finally uncovered some answers. Up until that point, I had never internalised how much I had always had to fight to compensate for the things I found difficult and the effort and energy it had sucked out of me. I had berated myself for years for all my difficulties and failings rather than being kind and understanding to myself for the effects it had had on my education.

I realised what a huge achievement it had been for me to even get through the education system, with the odds stacked against me. However, instead of feeling pride at my achievement, I felt I had paid a high price for the appearance of normality. I began grieving for the girl who fought like hell to appear like everyone else, who endured criticism after criticism, berating her for how intelligent but lazy she was. A teacher once wrote to my parents saying, "She is rapidly turning her laziness into a full time occupation." My heart bled for that little girl inside of me and for all kids who suffer like I did, spending their childhoods being criticised and feeling misunderstood.

I had hoped that with an ADHD diagnosis and a whole new range of drugs to try, I would find the magic cure. But that was not to be. After an official diagnosis from a new psychiatrist, I tried a bunch of previously unexplored medications and therapies. I enjoyed the energy, drive and focus I gained from taking stimulants. However, the side effects were awful, and I rapidly became dependent on stimulant medications to function - even just to get out of bed in the morning. When I wasn't on stimulants, I was self-medicating more than ever with caffeine and sugar. My ADHD brain had become so used to its dopamine fix, that without it, I felt useless again.

I spent a good few years trying any ADHD medication I could get my hands on. I was convinced that ADHD was the explanation for my depression and that a drug would be able to cure everything. I was to be sorely disappointed. Although some worked for periods of time, others became addictive, stopped working or the side-effects became too much. They did not cure my depression, they simply masked it and they definitely were not a long-term solution for my pain. I slowly began to realise that ADHD might have explained much about my school years and education struggles but trying to treat it in adulthood with a bunch of medications was not dealing with the depression from its root.

Addiction: An Escape
from Life & Pain

*"The attempt to escape from pain,
is what creates more pain."*
- Gabor Maté

I never thought I would ever experience addiction. The word "addict" conjured up images of people you might see in movies or read about in celebrity news. However, it was closer to home than I thought.

I became addicted to the ADHD medication, Adderall. For the first time in years, I felt normal. It felt like a heavy cloud had lifted and I was euphoric. The medicine let me experience happiness without my incessant ruminating and negative thoughts ruining everything. It let me escape from myself to a happy and carefree world that I never wanted to leave.

Adderall is an amphetamine. It began to make sense to me how someone could use addictive substances as a crutch. Drink, drugs or whatever the preferred 'poison', offers an alluring escape from a pained, tortured self. My poison was the medication - an escape from my life and my pain.

I heard Dr. Gabor Maté, physician and addiction expert, say that when he meets an addict, he congratulates them on finding something to keep them alive. Because yes, depression and suicide are the other option.

I enjoyed my Adderall high for some time, but after a few months, I began to need a higher dose to get the same feeling. And then an even higher dose. On the days when I did not take the pill, I could not get out of bed. I simply could not function. I was low and exhausted. I needed Adderall to do anything. I had to face it, I was addicted.

The decision to get off the drug wasn't easy, but I knew it had to happen. The withdrawal period was the most hellish few weeks of my life. I fully experienced what addicts must go through in order to detox from their drug. The tremors, brain zaps, mood swings, fatigue, aches, pains, anxiety, and depression. I was very close to checking myself into rehab.

So horrendous is the withdrawal process that for most addicts, staying on the drug for the rest of their lives seems the better option. I did consider it but, as I was becoming habituated to the medication, and needing to constantly increase the dose, I knew staying on it for the rest of my life was not a solution. I was already at the maximum dose that doctors would prescribe.

It was during that period that I changed my attitude to addiction. I realised there is no real difference between a depressive and an addict. Both are driven by an intense, internal pain that cannot be shaken. People who, for one reason or another, find it difficult to get through life, and need to call in some reinforcement. Drugs, alcohol and depression are all coping mechanisms some people use in order to survive.

In fact, when drunk, I had often joked that I should have been an alcoholic instead of a depressive. At least that way I would have a few moments of fun and happiness. I was kidding of course, but deep down I understood that depressives and addicts are often driven by the same internal torture. An innate discontentment with life. Depression and addiction were the coping mechanisms I used as I had strayed off path and lost touch with my true self.

My Life was a Bunch of Plasters

*"We are the sum of our actions, and therefore
our habits make all the difference."*
- Aristotle

O ne day, I realised that my life was a bunch of plasters (aka. band aids) piled one on top of the other. I was constantly plastering over some pain or another, avoiding myself and my negative emotions. I never really dealt with any of the issues. I just kept on covering up my pain with the next thing that could give me some slight relief.

A week of a strict detox diet made me realise how often I used food to avoid being with myself and my emotions. When I didn't sleep enough, I'd drink coffee. Feeling anxious? Reach for the chocolate. Too tired to get through the day? Have some caffeine. Feeling low? Eat some cake. Heavy head? Another coffee. And so on.

These plasters were addictions in disguise (or not so disguised).

Every hour or two I would put a plaster on a wound - on something that was bothering me. I never actually dealt with my tiredness, exhaustion, stress, or depression. Patching it up gave me relief for an hour or two until the next time I needed a patch up. Surely that wasn't healthy? Surely this vicious cycle would crash and burn at some stage? How long could I keep it up?

I wondered how many of us do this with sugar, coffee,

cigarettes, food, exercise, drugs, alcohol, shopping, work, studying or screens? How many of us are putting plasters on some emotions that we simply do not want to fully feel?

Like the medication to which I had become addicted, I could not sustain this either, so I checked myself into a no sugar, no caffeine, detox retreat. In the silence of my four walls at the sparsely furnished retreat, with none of my plasters there to prop me up, I realised how much I had been masking my feelings and emotions. I realised that I suffered with recurrent headaches and migraines - clearly stress-related - that I would 'treat' repeatedly with sugar, caffeine, or pills. Yet the headaches always returned. I kept putting plasters on the problems but never dealt with the underlying cause.

My awareness of what I was doing to myself grew on this retreat. I began to peel away the plasters and face up to reality, wanting to take more responsibility for the life I had created for myself. I knew it was time to stop patching up every feeling with a band-aid. I could no longer keep running, falling, and sticking on a plaster. I needed to take them all off and see what the hell was going on underneath.

After cutting out the plasters I became acutely aware of when I craved sugar or caffeine. The physical need had gone, but every time I experienced a craving, I would try to see what painful emotion I was attempting to avoid. Any slight feeling of stress, nervousness, or sadness, made me want to grab a chocolate or something sweet. To comfort, soothe and self-medicate. It is not by chance that these foods are called comfort foods. They help us avoid our discomfort and numb our emotions. I was perpetually on the run - literally all day long because I was subconsciously trying to avoid sitting still and feeling my feelings. All of them - including my pain and fear.

I now realise how crucial it is to sit and just *be*. To sit with our emotions rather than numb them. We are human *be*ings not human *do*ings. The Sabbath was intended as a day of rest. A day for us to simply be and not do. When I looked at my crazy hectic life, I was sure it wasn't intended to be like this. We need time to chill, to be with ourselves and to feel our feelings. This generation is the furthest from that. Technology does not allow us any down time. We seem to have reached a crisis point where we never just sit still and face our emotions and I was no exception.

Many of us have our addictions. They may not be commonly accepted or diagnosed as such, but they are all ways of distracting us from ourselves and our painful emotions. Addiction, like depression, is a coping mechanism. Something to fill that void inside of us. That life-sucking, emptiness deep inside that we cannot quite put our finger on. That lack of inner peace.

Addictions are our way of coping with negative feelings that we simply don't want to face. In truth, we are avoiding ourselves - our true essence. That bit deep inside that is yelling to be heard. That inner knowing that softly whispers what path we should follow, if only we would listen. I know because I ignored it for decades. Our souls are relentless, never giving up, pulling us towards our true path - the best possible path which will lead us to our highest potential.

Incessant, Endless & Hyperactive Thoughts

"You are wherever your thoughts are, make sure your thoughts are where you want to be."
- Rebbe Nachman of Breslov

Psychology studies and years of depression often had me wondering what makes us different from one another? Why can one person have it all and feel miserable whilst someone else who seems to have much less, glides happily through life? Is it just down to personality? Or is there more going on? It was clear to me that external factors are no indicator of happiness. Look at all those rich, famous, gorgeous, successful people who turn to drugs or suicide. They are clearly not happy.

So what is it that makes us happy? Is there some underlying system that we can't analyse? Our thoughts and beliefs about ourselves clearly play a role, but I didn't understand what it was.

My hyperactive thoughts were endless. Incessant. Relentless. And over the years, they got worse and worse. There were times when I wanted to hit myself over the head with a hammer just to stop the damn voices in my head. An endless stream of thoughts about how useless and worthless I was barraged me all day long. I was in a constant state of stress.

My head practically burst all day long with the things I had to do and the decisions I had to make.

In my mind I was a useless mother, bad wife, ungrateful daughter, and hopeless human being. My negative thoughts took over my life. I was only free of them in sleep. They were so debilitating that I simply could not get on with daily life. I was unable to accept that my thoughts may not actually be true. The reality and truth of the situation could not change the way my thoughts made me feel. If anyone tried to help or say something nice to me, I just felt worse about myself. I remember people trying to compliment me, but I was simply unable to hear them. My internal voice was too loud. It would always be there to scream out its counter-answer. My internal voice knew the truth - that I was useless and revolting.

As the years went by, I realised that a major cause of my angst were my own irrational, relentless thoughts. They filled me with fear and prevented me from living my life. I learnt the hard way that our thoughts determine everything.

There are treatments available that try to deal with our thoughts. Cognitive behavioural therapy confirmed that my thoughts were irrational. Coaching helped to reframe my thoughts and answer back to them. However, neither of these treatments could fully relieve me of these negative thoughts or cure my depression and anxiety. It got to a point where the berating voices in my head were so loud, so clear and so cruel that it felt like they weren't my own thoughts. As if they were external voices attacking me from the outside.

My thoughts were slowly killing me. I was desperate. I needed them to go away. I decided that a better way to deal with the incessant, hyperactive thoughts was to calm them down or quieten them somehow. I'd had enough of discussing and analysing them with therapists and coaches. I knew that once they were calmed, decision-making would be so much easier. Medication and traditional therapies had not helped. It was time for something different...

Meditation? You Must be Kidding!

"Silence is the maturation of wisdom."
-Maimonides

For fifteen years, people had tried to encourage me to meditate. It didn't appeal to me at all. As far as I was concerned meditation was some weird thing that monks and new agers did. It was crazy and foreign. I was simply not one of those odd, happy-clappy, chanting people sitting cross-legged on the floor.

Besides, suggesting that I meditate was ludicrous. I could not even shut up my hyperactive, crazy thoughts down for a few seconds. And I couldn't possibly contemplate sitting still. Even a trip to the cinema was a nightmare for me as I found it virtually impossible to sit still for long and only do one thing. Multitasking was my default mode - I never did just one thing at a time so how would I possibly manage to meditate?

So, I ignored the advice time and again. But after many years of more meds, more psychiatrists, and more psychologists, meditation was suggested again, and I thought I was finally ready to try. I downloaded a few meditation apps onto my phone and set a daily alarm to remind me to meditate. That alarm remained on my phone for a few more years and every single day I ignored it. It took several more years of depression and anxiety, with a couple of breakdowns thrown in before I succumbed.

I bumped into the only person I knew who meditated, and who had mentioned it to me fifteen years earlier and asked where I could go to get help. She recommended a yoga class which I ended up attending for a year. This yoga class was the beginning of my healing. It was the first time I deeply understood the concept that we don't have to identify with our thoughts.

While researching ADHD, I discovered that meditation is often recommended for patients to help them focus better. My ADHD diagnosis had led me to a new psychiatrist who also suggested meditation as a means of helping myself. The psychiatrist and his wife in fact ran meditation and mindfulness courses focused on reducing stress. Mindfulness Based Stress Reduction - MBSR courses are now widely recognised by the medical field. Nothing weird, woo-woo or Buddhist about it. No sitting on the floor required and medically and scientifically approved. I was still resistant but gave in and went along. Over a period of two years, I meditated frequently. Sitting still, trying not to get swept away by my incessant negative thoughts was pretty torturous. But despite seeing no results yet, I stuck with it. As far as I was concerned, I had tried everything else and this was my last hope.

What I discovered about meditation is that there is no right or wrong way to do it. It didn't matter if my thoughts were incessant and loud. Meditating simply required taking a step back and becoming aware of my thoughts from an observer's position. I was to notice each thought and let it float by without getting caught up in it, and without berating and judging myself. Thoughts did come into my head, but it was my choice whether or not I would attend to them and let them escalate.

I began to regularly take a step back and look at my thoughts from the outside. From this vantage point, I saw that I was not my thoughts and learned to watch them with detached amusement. I could notice them and say to myself, ``I am having a thought that xyz....''. For the first time in my life, I could look at my thoughts without identifying with them and without latching onto them. I also learnt to do the same with feelings, memories, bodily sensations and behavioural urges. I recognised them as being separate from me and I could release them without getting caught in a downward spiral.

One day, I downloaded a walking meditation app. This was easier for me as it allowed me to multitask. I was able to walk the dog, exercise, plus meditate! The App talked me through a fifteen-minute walk that taught me to notice the sights, sounds, smells, and physically feel the things in my environment. It was a revelation. It started to come more naturally to me the more I did it. Immersing myself in my surroundings forced me into the present moment which caused my hyperactive thoughts to shut up for a while. I could concentrate only on what I was doing at that moment, focusing on my senses and perceptions. Suddenly the trees and flowers popped out and looked more vibrant and beautiful than I had ever known them to be.

Another surprising mindful moment came whilst sitting on the beach alone, relaxing and enjoying the sensations. I suddenly discovered I was feeling and hearing myself breathing deeply. I was totally focused on this deep, relaxed breathing. Is this what meditation feels like, I wondered? I was amazed at how relaxed I suddenly felt. It was then that I realised that the beach virtually forces mindfulness. With its all-encompassing sights and sounds, it encourages and forces us to be present and in the moment. You simply can't help but experience all the natural elements around you, engaging all your senses. The powerful sound of the sea. The hot sun beating on your skin. The strong breeze ruffling your hair and cooling your face. The smells. The salty taste on your lips. The glistening ocean and soft shimmering sand. Your senses are overwhelmed, and you have to spend time in the present moment.

The mindfulness course taught that true joy happens in the present moment. The most precious moments are the ones when we are present. Sport, nature, and the like. Cycling, for example, used to take me out of thinking mode as it immersed me in the intensity of the experience. I did not realise it at the time, but that was mindfulness.

I noticed that over the years I had often turned to creative or calming activities. Activities that were meditative in nature, although I did not realise that was what drew me to them. Crafting, crocheting, drawing, painting, music, writing and exercise.

I persisted with meditation even though I had no big shifts or results (yet). It was a huge struggle but I saw how necessary it was. And I persisted for my family. I guess I still had hope. I was desperate to experience all the benefits people claimed it could bring me.

I felt as though God had led me to meditation (well, had tried to for years!). It is something so many of us need in this day and age of overwhelm and smartphones. I began to feel closer to God and closer to my true self, not to my mask.

Suddenly, I hit rock bottom. A major depressive episode. The worst I'd experienced in my life. I tried a series of new medications. I lay in bed on my forty-third birthday and was given the only two gifts my family thought suited someone as lost in depression as I was - a headband to monitor meditation, and a breathing-monitor to help slow my breathing and reduce anxiety. Not your typical birthday gifts. But things were that bad. Nothing could bring me even the tiniest bit of joy. My family knew a regular gift would be futile and insulting to me.

Rock Bottom

"There is no greater disease than the loss of hope."
-Rabbi Yisroel Salanter

Sometimes we need to hit rock bottom in order to make a genuine change. We have to experience the darkness before being able to accept and experience the light. We must break down, reaching our lowest point to learn to surrender and give up the need for control. And to break our addiction to fear and be ready and willing to forgive ourselves and others.

When a person hits rock bottom they are desperate. Ready to change. Ready to choose to do things differently. We need to decide that we are ready to heal, ready to transform, ready to grow before any meaningful change can occur.

It is extremely painful to move out of our comfort zone, our conditioning, and our regular patterns. Especially the destructive ones. It involves great strength and, often, a lot of pain, for a person to become ready to break the patterns. I had finally come to that point.

I had sunk into such a deep bout of depression that I took myself away from daily life. I found myself sitting on a bed in a strange hotel in an utter state of panic. My body was tense, I was having palpitations, I felt sick deep in the pit of my stomach and my neck was sore from tension. I had booked a massage and was panicking about how I was going to fit in a shower, walk on the beach and eat breakfast in a local cafe before my massage. I'm even embarrassed to write this.

Suddenly, I realised the craziness of my irrational anxiety and began to laugh out loud. And then sob hysterically. The situation must be pretty dire if I am so anxious about such things. I was suddenly able, for the first time, to step back and see clearly how irrational and out of control my anxiety was. Up until that moment, I always rationalised my anxiety, believing it to be a justified response to the events that life presented to me. Now I could see it for what it was. And here I sat, at rock bottom, fully aware that there was no other problem apart from a major anxiety and depression issue.

I knew that I couldn't go on living this way. I saw no way out and no way of continuing either. My anxiety was at an all-time high, and my depression had engulfed me. There were days when I would lie naked on the floor for forty minutes at a time, unable to pick myself up and get in the shower.

Something needed to change. How much more could I take of this? I had tried everything. I had to finally resign myself to the fact that there wasn't going to be a magic cure that would erase years and years of suffering and ensure it would never come back. But that is what I wanted more than anything. I wanted to live a normal life. Or else die. Carrying on like this wasn't an option anymore.

I kept trying to meditate. I concentrated on deep breathing for five minutes and then spent the rest of the day mostly unaware that I was automatically breathing deeply. Every time I noticed my deep-breathing, I realised this is what God wants from me. To be here. Present. Living. God wants me to be my true self, the real me. Not the *me* caught up in endless rumination about who or what I should be. I needed to stop with the incessant thoughts and just *be*. Then I would be able to emerge into my true identity. I needed to strip off all the masks and layers and be who I was, who I am. How could that not be what God wants? But how would I ever get there?

I somehow knew that this dip into deep depression was going to be different to the others. It was going to change me. I would never be the same again. Not just in the sense that I needed to slow down, look after myself and reduce stress, but something fundamental was going to change. And when I was able to be mindful by breathing or walking, I knew that this was the place I had to keep myself in. To stay out of the tornado going on in my mind.

I had tried virtually every drug and talk therapy. I was aware that my self-limiting beliefs were destroying me, and that therapies and other interventions had not managed to replace and remove these damaging beliefs and thoughts that were sitting deep in my subconscious.

God, Where Are You?

"An individual should hold an awareness
of God and His love all the
time. He should not separate his consciousness
from the Divine while he journeys on the way,
nor when he lies down nor when he rises up."
- Nahmanides

I grew up as an observant, modern-orthodox Jew but a part of me always felt that I belonged to a Godless religion. I hate saying it, but that is how it felt to me. Keeping many of the commandments, performing the rituals, festivals/holidays, Sabbath, and the rest - it just felt ritualistic to me. I couldn't feel God in it. There was no spirituality in the way I experienced my religion. No connection to the Divine.

Praying became so habitual and routine that it lost all meaning. Especially because I prayed in a language that was not my mother tongue. I barely understood what I said when I prayed. I followed commandments out of habit, and if I'm honest, fear. I believed there would be punishment and retribution for not adhering to the letter of the law.

To get through this life and my suffering, I wanted to feel God in my everyday life. I needed to sense a reason for it all. My observance wasn't enough. Religion, the way I was practising it, wasn't connecting me. The spirituality simply wasn't there.

A big part of me was jealous of people who hadn't grown up

observant - who chose to become religious from a deep desire to connect. That made so much more sense. To be religious from a place of choice and connection.

I didn't feel Divine presence, but I did believe that things happen for a reason. I tried to remember that there is a bigger picture. I wanted to constantly remember that the Divine is there above us - watching, guiding, loving, sending signs and messages, wanting us to connect and to find and fulfill our mission in this world.

Being a believing Jew and even an observant one was the easy bit. Actually talking about spirituality or a connection to the Divine seemed scarier. It simply wasn't what I was used to. In fact, it seemed rather absurd or embarrassing to me to be so trusting in a higher power, or to believe that the Divine might be sending us guidance.

My first encounter with someone spiritual was aged twenty at University. He truly believed in God. None of his religion was for anyone else, nor because he ought to, nor because he cared what others thought of him. He had a real relationship with the Divine and I was envious.

My modern orthodox Jewish way was not only devoid of spirituality but definitely devoid of mysticism. We never spoke about souls, the afterlife or anything from Kabbalah. That was a big no-no. I believed I wasn't religious or worthy enough to study Kabbalah. Rules like women shouldn't study Kabbalah and one needs to be over forty to study it, were so ingrained in me that I simply didn't go near it.

From the depths of despair, after weeks in bed during this deep depression, it came to me that perhaps my depression is the challenge God gave me. Maybe God was using depression as a means to wake me up to something?

I prayed and asked to feel God in my everyday life. To know that there is a bigger picture and a reason for everything. I was truly suffering, and meaningless suffering is especially hard to bear.

PART 2

AWAKENING

Then I Met Michele

"I am personally convinced that one person can be a change catalyst, a 'transformer' in any situation, any organization. Such an individual is yeast that can leaven an entire loaf. It requires vision, initiative, patience, respect, persistence, courage, and faith to be a transforming leader."
-Stephen Covey

I felt like I had tried everything. I was at rock bottom. I had crashed. Months in bed. I honestly didn't know how I could go on living like that. I didn't believe there was going to suddenly be some magical medication or therapy that was going to change my life around. I didn't know how I was going to be able to get through the rest of my life. I never planned to end my life, but I really did want to die and to end it all. I wished for some terminal illness to end my suffering. Deep down though, I knew that wasn't going to happen. I was here for a reason and God wasn't going to get rid of me until I had done what I was here for.

I randomly went to a meditation class with a close friend. Her cousin, Michele was a meditation teacher and was coming to our town. I got dragged along as her only friend that meditated.

I found the class that evening hard as ever, but something made me want to go back for more. Michele claimed that through her chakra meditation you can clear out blockages from your energy centres and become your true, authentic self. That really spoke to me! I was so fed up with my masks. I didn't know much about chakras, something to do with Yoga and Buddhism or Hinduism, I thought. I felt a bit uneasy as a Jew, but I had heard it being said that chakras are like the sefirot in Kabbalah so that kind of made it "Kosher". I decided to meet Michele one on one to try to get a handle on this meditation thing once and for all. I clearly wasn't quite getting it in my solo attempts, so a guide would be just what I needed.

Everything changed after my third session with Michele. She led me through a guided meditation and did some sort of shadow/inner child work with me. It involved taking me back to a trauma in childhood, feeling the emotions and feelings from that time and nurturing and comforting my inner child. From the start, Michele had been telling me to write down my thoughts, but I hadn't done so. That day, however, I felt a powerful compulsion to write. It felt as if I was on the cusp of something huge. Something that I absolutely had to document. Something different. Something I had resisted and rejected for so long. I was a skeptic, a cynic, but something was happening here, and I felt I was changing from normal to 'woo'.

I felt amazing. I can only describe it as some kind of heavenly bliss. It was like a switch had been flicked and I was no longer remotely anxious or depressed. I was having a spiritual awakening and I realised that my life was never going to be the same again. Seventeen years of therapies and medications had not come close to helping me like this. I needed to understand what was going on.

Awakening to Something New

*"God arranged creation so that even while in
the physical world, man would be able to open
a door to the spiritual and experience the
Divine."*
-Rabbi Aryeh Kaplan

There is no other way to put it. Despite being a complete non-believer in 'woo-woo', it was apparent to me that I had experienced a spiritual awakening and a brief glimpse of enlightenment.

Enlightenment has been defined as the intellectual understanding of higher religious principles. A state of perfect knowledge combined with infinite compassion. It is an understanding of the way things appear to us and the true nature of these same appearances. This includes our own minds as well as the external world. This knowledge is the basic antidote to ignorance and suffering.

Awakening is a shift in consciousness to a perception of reality that has previously been unrealised. A new awareness of reality is born and suddenly you can see more of this world: the parts we could not see before. Call it, the spiritual realm.

Had it not been for the fact that I had seen Eckhart Tolle on Oprah once, I might have thought I was going crazy. In fact, I imagine that some people who have a spiritual awakening and don't know what it is, must think something is very wrong with them. But I knew I wasn't ill. In fact, I knew I was mentally very right. It was the most right I had felt in years.

I realised that what I had experienced was similar to what I heard people sometimes describe as a Near Death Experience (NDE). And that what I had felt, seemed to offer a taste of what people go through at the end of life. Some people have also reported having such shifts in consciousness following severe illnesses, accidents, or other major life-changing events. These experiences transform the landscape of our lives instantaneously.

How do you describe a spiritual awakening? There is no language for it on Earth. The spiritual realm and God are essentially inexplicable in earthly terms. But I will try.

It felt as if there was a huge, powerful, white light source above my head showering unconditional love, bliss, and inner peace on me. It seemed clear to me that this source of light was what people refer to as God, The Creator or Source. I was filled with a huge sense of awe. Not fear at all - but pure wonder, amazement, and reverence.

Every time I closed my eyes, I fell immediately into a deep, relaxing, blissful, meditative state. It felt like there was a whole other world behind my eyelids. Like a huge cinema screen had opened up behind them. Like my eyes were open even when they were closed.

I felt a major shift. A sense of wholeness and completeness and a state of blissful inner peace. My breathing slowed right down. It was deep and hoarse.

I was freaked out and excited. Scared and relieved. Worried and curious. I was entering a whole new journey with no idea where it was going to take me.

Beforehand, I would not have been able to really explain what consciousness was, but it was clear to me that my state of consciousness had altered and expanded. I had experienced a shift in perception where the ordinary world became extraordinary. I had an expanded, zoomed out awareness. Whereas normally I had five senses, I now felt I had been given an extra sense. I can't explain exactly what it was, but in the same way that our senses give us information about reality, I now seemed to be getting new information about reality but from a different sense. The new sense gave me an understanding of how and why things are in this world. In the same way that I can see a chair and *know* it is a chair, or hear a bell and *know* it is a bell - I felt like I had extra sense that was giving me absolute knowledge.

I use the terminology of being certain and knowing things because that is how it felt to me, like I was given an extra sense that gave me knowledge in no uncertain terms.

I became intensely relaxed and in a state of full, inner peace. I knew that everything in life was really, really okay and exactly as it should be. There was no space for regrets about the past or any anxiety or negative feelings whatsoever. I felt complete bliss. It was very reassuring, and I realised that this state of expanded consciousness is obviously what many people enter as they near the end of their life: a sense of peace, serenity, and acceptance. Otherwise they would surely be in a state of anxiety. As their consciousness expands, they are given the ability to see, feel or sense the bigger picture and are overwhelmed with a wonderful feeling of calmness and understanding. I found it very comforting to know that this amazing blissful feeling is what one feels upon leaving this world. If only people knew, they would not be so afraid of death. The feeling was Divine.

I also knew death wasn't the end. I became hyper aware of my soul as the true *me*. My eternal soul that existed before this physical body and that exists after it leaves this body. I understood that this physical body, name, and personality, is not the real me. And that my soul has existed through many other lifetimes.

My awareness, my consciousness had expanded. I was aware that my life, on this Earth, as Britt, was such a tiny part of the big scale of *me*. That there is so much more my soul has experienced than just this lifetime. It was as if someone had zoomed out my life. Like when you zoom out on a map on the computer and suddenly what seemed like a large city is less than a tiny dot in the context of the whole wide world. I realised there is so much more than just this short lifetime. That we exist across many lifetimes and that this lifetime is but a mere dot in the larger scale of my existence. I felt that nothing is worth getting anxious about, because in the scheme of things, it is like a miniscule dot.

My clinical depression disappeared. **And never came back.** The realisation that our existence in this world, our very lives, are intricately planned out to help us learn and experience what we are here to learn and experience suddenly became so clear. Nothing that would normally be perceived as upsetting or negative bothered me. I could now sense a bigger picture, a bigger plan which made everything in my life instantly more bearable. I *knew* that everything was for the best. Even things I used to view as upsetting or tragic. I simply knew that every event and occurrence was for a reason. I wasn't just trying to convince myself - my new 'sixth' sense was making me experientially feel and absolutely *know* it.

Even the thought of death, mine or someone I loved, didn't change the intense knowing that it would still be okay. I was overcome with the feeling that death is never a tragedy. Interestingly, I later discovered there is no Hebrew word for tragedy because apparently when we leave this world and finally know the truth - we get to know that nothing is a tragedy, but part of a bigger plan.

I felt a detachment from stress. Nothing and no one could ruffle or annoy me. I had an overwhelming sense of love and connection with everything and everyone. I saw through to their pure good souls. There was a sense of Oneness. That we are all a spark of God. All part of the One. I could feel this Oneness and Divine presence in everything. I suddenly understood that each of us is truly the same. Irrelevant of race, religion, colour, gender, nationality etc. That we are all part of the One.

I realised that we are pure, good souls, sparks of God who have come into flawed and imperfect human bodies and personalities, with the aim of working on life lessons and overcoming challenges. I wondered how I could possibly blame or judge anyone for their imperfections when we all, without exception, have things we need to work on and fix about ourselves?

I became very patient with people in situations that would ordinarily have annoyed or stressed me. I felt total love, understanding and compassion for everyone. I saw everyone as the same, as equal. As a soul. I felt I could see through to the pure good soul of every person I met, even if their behaviour was appalling. I would simply be filled with pure unconditional love, non-judgement, and compassion for them. Knowing that their behaviour wasn't their true self but came from a place of pain and fear. I found it quite bizarre and even surprised myself with how understanding and non-judgmental I was.

My life entered a flow state. It felt like there was an intelligent energy moving and manipulating my life. I no longer felt alone. My life was being guided by a higher power. I felt total trust in that higher power and no need to be anxious or control life anymore. I began to see and feel supernatural signs, synchronicities and messages that were clearly more than coincidental but seemed to hide behind nature.

I also began to feel that although we do have an element of free will, much of what goes on in this world is controlled and managed by the Divine. That we simply need to have trust and faith rather than feeling like a victim. Because everything in this world is part of a Divine plan. I no longer believe in accidents or coincidences.

It felt like this world is a computer game where I control my character. That I don't need to get totally immersed in my character because I am aware that she is not the true me. The true me is a soul who has the controls to the character and can decide what she does. The real me has just come to play this role for a few decades. Knowing this, I felt a sense of detachment, which stopped me from getting caught up in drama or stress. I found myself fully trusting in God and the Divine plan.

I was living totally in the present moment. Not ruminating about the past, nor stressing about the future and not getting caught up in hyperactive thoughts. I was constantly aware of my deep breathing and felt the need for more silence. I could suddenly see the beauty in nature like I had never seen before. Colours popped out and it seemed like my sense of vision was enhanced.

And then came the realisation that this blissful feeling of enlightenment that I was feeling, this state of expanded consciousness, is our goal. That this is what the redemption will be like. That this is what people will feel in the Messianic era. That what I had always referred to as the Moshiach (Messiah) or redemption is the same as Buddhists would call enlightenment or Christians would call salvation. I understood that this is what we are aiming for. Enlightenment is the end goal. And meditation is key to achieving this state of consciousness.

As quickly as my 'superpowers' came, they went away. However thankfully, not fully. They left a residual knowledge that my world would never be the same. The feelings I felt were not my natural state, but they were like an invisible beacon showing me what I had to strive to get back to. I could view people with compassion. I could access the feeling that we are all interconnected souls: sparks of God. That knowledge altered my behaviour. Things that would normally stress me out, no longer propelled me into a state of anxiety. If I was running late because of traffic, instead of going into my usual state of anxiety, I would become aware that this was happening for a reason. Sometimes I would see and feel the reasons, but usually not. I would simply know everything that happens is for a reason and is in some way for my good, for the benefit of my personal growth. We are all here to learn, grow and evolve.

I knew this world is not supposed to be about fear. God is unconditional love. We, as sparks of God, are also meant to attain a state of unconditional love for all. There is no place for fear, guilt, shame, and hatred where we are headed. I became acutely aware that my thoughts create my reality and that I needed to change my negative thought patterns and the negative emotions that were holding me back. I knew that the key to living in that state of peace was to live every moment in the present. And that focusing on the breath, is a pathway into the present moment.

Meditation is the tool that we have in order to reach spiritual heights and yet it has been taken out of religion for many. I hadn't been seeking spirituality, I only turned to meditation to escape my pervasive depression. But I was suddenly able to connect with the Divine realm in a way I had never been able to through prayer. I felt the ability for my prayers and intentions to be answered and to manifest in a way that conventional prayer had never enabled.

I had experienced a glimpse of enlightenment. It was the most beautiful and unbelievable experience, but I could barely understand what had happened to me. I began to read books, websites, anything I could get my hands on - in an attempt to learn what it was all about. It didn't take long to discover that it is not just Buddhist monks experiencing spiritual awakenings. There are shifts in consciousness happening all over the world, even to those neither searching nor meditating. It was evident to me that without my consciously seeking it, I had very suddenly been fast-tracked onto a spiritual journey.

Sudden & Unexpected Changes

Progress is impossible without change, and those who
cannot change their minds cannot change anything.
-George Bernard Shaw

During the period of time following my awakening, several sudden changes occurred.

Overnight I became a vegetarian, in fact almost vegan. That feeling of oneness, interconnectedness, love and compassion for everything and everyone in this world included animals. It was something I had always felt to some extent, but this jolt confirmed it. Expanded consciousness meant feeling the oneness with animals and therefore the idea of cruelty to them felt very wrong. There were times when I could hardly bear to be near someone eating meat or fish, as if I could feel the animal's pain. And there were other times when I felt a more contracted consciousness and was tempted to eat some meat, able to switch off my thoughts of where it came from. It doesn't surprise me that there are so many vegans in the world nowadays. As one's consciousness expands, it it is often a natural consequence.

I also felt a much deeper connection to the environment, and after years of being the queen of disposable dishes, I suddenly felt a need to look after this planet. This included a desire to stop using throw-away plastics and to start using more ecological, natural products rather than harsh chemicals. I felt that we weren't looking after the planet the way we are meant to. I also found myself not wanting to use pharmaceutical drugs and wanting to use more natural alternatives. And suddenly I was less interested in material things and the material world and had a strong desire to declutter and simplify my life.

My body also did a major reset during that period. My clinical depression and anxiety disappeared instantaneously along with their accompanying physical symptoms. Furthermore, other physical ailments that I had been suffering with began to clear up too. My digestive system did a self-detox. I spent a weekend vomiting and having severe diarrhea, during which I bizarrely felt perfectly fine. It felt like my body was clearing itself out. After the purging, I suddenly was unable to tolerate many of the things I was used to consuming. Coffee, sugar, alcohol, and processed foods were suddenly repellent to me, as if my body was guiding me toward a healthier diet.

As my body and behaviors were being reset, I realised that I was being drawn back to basics. I was being encouraged to look after the planet, avoid processed foods and man-made chemical substances and to recognise that we have an innate ability to heal ourselves.

Along with my general anxiety, several life-long phobias disappeared, and I understood that we are not meant to be living life from a place of fear.

Overnight, I shifted politically from being right-wing to left - in particular with regard to Israel and its security. I had been living in a state of fear and anxiety but now I was shifting over to a place dominated by love. I knew, deeply within myself, that we shouldn't be hurting or killing each other, that despite culture, race or religion we are actually all the same. Each of us is a soul, all equal, all part of the same One. It was shocking, but not unpleasantly so, to find myself so changed overnight in my opinions, without any thought process.

I was forced to practice radical truth-telling. I could barely tolerate what was out of alignment with my soul, my true self. Seeing people, going places, conversations. Suddenly I was unable to betray my own truth and do things that were not right for me. I had no choice but to listen to my inner truth, because not listening to it made me feel viscerally bad and uncomfortable. I was powerless to resist the intuitive guidance I was receiving from within myself.

I became aware of a subtle cause and effect and the need to keep my behaviour impeccable. A couple of times I felt an immediate karmic reaction if I erupted in anger or unkindness. It was like I had a heightened mind-body connection often with an immediate cause and effect. If my thoughts, words, or actions were not pure, loving and compassionate, I would feel painful ramifications on my body. I quickly learned to work hard on my character traits to make sure my intentions were good and pure. I understood that we are meant to emulate God, being loving and compassionate at all times, even in our thoughts. Otherwise we feel the repercussions often in this world and lifetime.

I also became aware of how my thoughts create my reality and realised my focused attention could manifest things. I explored this concept and discovered the law of attraction. It dawned on me that my years of depression had me focused in a downward spiral of negative thinking that allowed me to stay there.

Experiencing emotions shifted radically within me. Instead of getting caught up in emotions, they seemed to wash through me. I sat with them, without ignoring or suppressing them, not feeling a need to feed them, ruminate and get all caught up in them. I could no longer suppress emotions. I cried when I needed to cry. Emotions began to pass through me very naturally, like a wave.

I discovered negative emotions had to be processed. I would find myself consciously searching inside myself for the source of the issue and begin to process and remove it. Negative emotions repeated themselves over and over for me to grasp the lessons I was supposed to derive from them. Each time I didn't grasp the lesson, a similar learning opportunity would rear its head until I learned it and began to deal with it. Negative emotions were powerfully reflected in my body. I could step back from them and ask myself why I was feeling this in my body. A new freedom came with the ability to recognise the emotions behind my body sensations, acknowledge, breathe through and release them.

For a significant period of time, I felt very much like I was floating and was not really present in my body. I now understand that this is being spiritually ungrounded. We are spiritual beings, but it is essential that our spirit, our soul, is grounded in this Earth. I have since discovered that this is also a concept within psychology and that there are grounding techniques to assist when feeling ungrounded, dissociated, or anxious.

My intuition opened up in the form of what felt like guidance from the spiritual realm. Hunches, gut feelings, inspirations and messages flowed into my life. Somehow, I knew what to do without the need for decision making and without using my rational, thinking brain. I learned to trust my intuition, recognizing it as a bridge between the physical and spiritual worlds. I trusted that I was being guided from a higher realm. I had understood that meditation helps one connect to their intuition, but I had not expected this. When I prayed or asked for things, I felt guided to the answers. Guidance arrived in numerous forms including feelings, experiences, dreams, and thoughts.

A Spiritual What?!

"The spiritual journey is individual, highly personal. It can't be organized or regulated. It isn't true that everyone should follow one path. Listen to your own truth."
- Ram Dass

Prior to this awakening, I had no idea what a Spiritual Journey was. As far as I was concerned, I had my God and my religion and that was that. I had heard of spiritual journeys from watching the movie Eat, Pray, Love, but I can't say I really related to it. I didn't connect meditating as anything to do with God in the slightest and I had only turned to meditation as a last resort to get me out of my deep, hellish depression. All the research seemed to claim it helped - not that they could explain why. I certainly didn't think I was connecting to God or doing anything spiritual in my earlier practices of meditation. But that day I just got it. I saw that meditation can take you to a deeply spiritual place - to the Divine.

Beforehand, I never quite understood why people on a spiritual journey were so involved in personal growth. Surely a spiritual journey was about connecting to God not about connecting to yourself and your selfish desires? I then realised that our true inner self, our soul, is a spark of God. So, connecting to ourselves and therefore being and living as our true self is connecting to that spark of God within us. It is what we are meant to do. It isn't selfish at all. Nor is it simply *only* personal growth and development. It is in fact, a deeply spiritual endeavour and it is what we are here, on this Earth, to do.

As the late Wayne Dyer said, "you are a spiritual being having a temporary human experience". I had heard it many times before but never really grasped it. I did now. Kabbalah teaches that this world is just a tiny fraction of what is really going on. What is the rest? There is a whole spiritual realm that we can't perceive. We are spiritual beings in a human body, souls that existed before we were born into this body and that will continue to exist after this physical body dies. We interpret the world through the medium of our physical bodies, and our five senses, but in actual fact we are much more than a body, and there are more than five senses.

Like myself, many people are now on a spiritual path. The journey of connecting to our soul, finding out who we really are and what we are here for. Our souls are here on this Earth for a reason. And our souls are pulling at us to become true to ourselves and to what we are here to do and learn.

We get so caught up in the nitty gritty details of this world that we often lose sight of the individual journey that each one of us must undertake. We are all here for a reason, whether or not we like it, and whether or not we are aware of it. Our soul has come into our body to evolve and improve itself in the time it has on this physical Earth. Many of us plod through life pretty unaware of why we are here, who we truly are and what this world is all about.

I had always desperately wanted to understand what this world is about. Furthermore, from as young as I can remember, I felt a deep urge to identify my role and purpose here. I knew that I wasn't here by chance, that

I was born to do something. But I never found what that was and had all but given up. Evidently though, my soul did know, and it kept on pulling and nudging at me until I finally listened. This awakening was part of it. And so, looking back, I have no regrets. I realise that I needed to go through what I did to get to where I am now. My depression, awakening and everything I experienced was all part of the Divine plan for me.

Hush-Hush Surrounding the Woo

"Three things cannot be long hidden: the
sun, the moon, and the truth."
- Buddha

I came to realise that for myself and others, spiritual experiences had been an unmentionable subject. Since we can't experience spiritual matters with our five senses, it is virtually impossible for us to access a true understanding of them. My previous default response to all spiritual occurrences was to laugh them off. That included anything supernatural, out of body experiences, dreams, miracles, and other 'unexplainable' phenomena.

Here I was, after having this unbelievable, spontaneous, spiritual awakening, with nowhere to turn. I desperately needed support and guidance. I felt people didn't understand me. Their eyes glazed over and I quickly realised that I wasn't able to talk about this with everyone. That is, unless I wanted people to think I'd gone crazy.

Spirituality, the spiritual realm, the supernatural and the paranormal, felt taboo. I could joke about something being straight from God rather than a coincidence, but I had never really believed it.

I barely discussed an out of body experience I had during childbirth as it was clear to me that people wouldn't really understand. And here I was again feeling utterly alone with an experience I was unable to share.

Synchronicities, signs and messages from the spiritual realm, angels or departed loved ones were never talked about. But as I gradually opened up my experiences to more people, I discovered that despite it being taboo, plenty of people had incidents that they had not readily divulged, tried to ignore or put down to nature or coincidence.

After my father-in-law died, I distinctly felt he sent us a couple of messages the day of his funeral. We had laughed them off as strange coincidences. I then read somewhere that spirits often try to send their loved ones messages to let them know they are ok and still around. I have mentioned this to a few friends who then proceeded to relay stories of the days following their loved ones death and the so called 'coincidences', or paranormal events they experienced.

I used to brush off dreams as meaningless too. I now realise that dreams are the spiritual realm communicating with us through our subconscious and trying to help us on our path here on Earth.

I now also realise that it's probable that many great thinkers, artists and teachers were spiritually awake. Their inspiration came through them from higher realms often during a 'flow' state. So many people who have blessed us with their science, art or music have acknowledged that their ideas came suddenly and will describe how the inspiration flowed through them - that they have in essence channeled their inspiration from the Divine realm.

The Empirical World That I Knew

*"To defy the authority of empirical evidence
is to disqualify oneself as someone worthy
of critical engagement in a dialogue."*
- Dalai Lama

I was excited to go back to my psychiatrist. I couldn't wait to tell him everything about my breakthrough. My depression and anxiety of almost 20 years had disappeared overnight. He was the one who had introduced me to meditation through the MBSR course (Mindfulness Based Stress Reduction) he and his wife ran. The course teaches meditation in a medical and scientific way without any spiritual component. I was so excited to thank him and tell him I was no longer depressed and that I wanted to come off my antidepressants. I was convinced that here was at least one person who would understand that meditation is a very spiritual experience and that it helped me to connect directly with the non-physical realm. After all, it was he who encouraged and taught me how to meditate.

My psychiatric appointment had been made months in advance and I bounded into his office and watched his eyes widen with delight as I told him I was feeling great. Let's face it, I had spent the last few years going to him with no good news. I was one of his treatment-resistant hopeless cases. However, as I began to explain to him my experience as best I could, I realised that he wasn't getting it. His eyes glazed over, and he had a blank expression on his face. I told him that I wanted to come off my medications. He didn't advise it. He thought I was just having a good patch and he would see me again in a couple of months. I wanted him to realise that meditation is totally a spiritual experience, but he had no clue what I was talking about.

I walked out of his office dejected. It was then that I realised that if the person who introduced me to meditation didn't understand or believe my experience, I needed to be very careful who I talk to about this stuff. People are going to think I've lost the plot. I even heard that people have ended up in psychiatric institutions after having spiritual awakenings. I decided that I shouldn't be telling everyone about it (so I decided to write a book!?). I never went back to my psychiatrist and I came off the meds myself. (Warning: I would NOT advise others to do this!)

I discovered eventually that what I had experienced was unusual. Most people get the benefits of meditation gently and slowly over time. Hence relieving anxiety and depression but without them knowing why or how, and without them realising that it is a spiritual experience. Bit by bit their consciousness expands, and they reap the benefits. I had a huge expansion of my consciousness all at once and got to see the whole world from a very wide perspective.

My first Psychology class at University was about evidence-based research: empirical evidence. And here I was with my own empirical evidence, the undeniable truth of my spiritual experience. But it didn't feel enough. People want proper, measurable research and statistics. Spiritual phenomena can't give that. Spiritual experiences need to be felt and experienced rather than analysed and examined. I knew that my experience was very real but that people might not be able, or ready, to hear or believe it. In fact, I myself was barely able and ready to believe it.

Understandably research into the spiritual realm must be fairly limited because science can't fully access the Divine and the spiritual ways of the world. So it sticks to what it can give evidential proof for. And spiritual occurrences is not it. Thanks to the internet, in the months that followed my awakening, I discovered many others have had similar experiences to me. I still kept relatively quiet and was hesitant to talk about it. Science doesn't have much room for spirituality. Illnesses, coincidences, paranormal, supernatural occurrences are all put down to some scientific, logical reasoning. But my eyes had been opened (more accurately my senses, or some weird new sense) to a whole new world. I had a new understanding and explanation for everything going on around me.

PART 3

ANALYSIS & INSIGHTS

The Analysis Begins

God cannot be compared to anything. Note this.
-Maimonides

I needed answers. I was excited and freaked out. I needed to understand what was going on, what had happened to me and why. I was a skeptic and cynic, remember?!

Through meditation and inner child-work with Michele, it was evident I had managed to clear some blockage from my system. I now had first-hand, experiential evidence of this energy clearing stuff working. However, all this chakra and energy business still sounded like gobbledygook to me.

I could no longer deny it all existed, and so I began to read up. I tried to grasp the concept that everything in this world is energy, which vibrates at different frequencies. I learnt that emotions are also energy which can get stuck and cause blockages, and negative emotions vibrate at a lower frequency than positive emotions.

If these understandings about energy, vibrations and blockages are really true and this is the way the world and our bodies really work, what else would that mean? Where would I go from there? What else would that lead me to believe in? Everything I had ever thought was starting to break away and I was learning anew. I was willing to entertain anything that I could understand and believe through my own deductive reasoning and experience.

I then read something that spoke to me. If you try to explain to a blind person something that they have never seen with their own eyes, they believe you. Just because they haven't experienced colour, or sky or clouds, doesn't mean that it isn't there. There are many things in this world that people would have never believed until science suddenly proved its existence. We do not actually need to see or experience something to believe it. In fact, believing can help you see and experience things. This analogy encouraged me to begin to calm down my cynical thinking, although my analytical brain was still on overdrive...

It is all There in Kabbalah

*The essence of the Redemption depends
upon learning Kabbalah*
-Vilna Gaon

E very time I would experience or understand something new, I would become skeptical and wonder if a source for this idea could be found in Judaism. I was repeatedly pointed towards Kabbalah - that secret body of wisdom I had grown up barely believing in and thinking I was barred from. Judaism states that Kabbalah contains a wealth of spiritual knowledge and wisdom, but it is only available to those who are ready to receive it.

Today I understand that Kabbalah is the blueprint for life, the mystical aspect of the Torah which contains all the hidden meanings about the world and answers philosophical questions about life: Who am I? What is the meaning of life? Where are we from? Why are we here? All the questions I had been seeking answers to. It gives practical and meditative tools designed to help us access higher states of consciousness opening a window through which all of reality can be perceived. It removes the blindfold and enables the spiritual world to be perceived. Kabbalah also had all the answers to explain what I had gone through.

We are so used to our physical realities that we tend to forget there is more, and hence don't feel its absence. We can't envision something we haven't experienced. Kabbalah teaches practical ways to perceive the spiritual realms, and by accessing higher states of consciousness, we can achieve greater levels of happiness and feel more fulfilled. It removes fear by enforcing the knowledge that everything in the world operates according to the Divine plan. This describes exactly what I felt when I had my awakening.

Kabbalah means to receive. It shows us the way to 'receive' the spiritual world that cannot be readily accessed through the five senses. A purpose of Kabbalah is to reveal the Divine in the physical world. Kabbalah teaches us how to activate our sixth sense that lies dormant until consciously awakened. The dormant sense that had suddenly activated in me.

In the Zohar, a central Kabbalistic text, God is referred to as Infinite Light. This description deeply reflects what I had sensed during my awakening. I now believe God to be the source of all energy - both the creator and the sustainer of all life.

Meditation techniques in Kabbalah are taught to consciously channel God's blessing and beneficence into the world to allow Divine light to flow down and enabling us to become a channel through which pours God's benevolence. However, there are 'klippot', negative layers or barriers stopping us from reaching our own perfection and in turn, bringing the world to perfection. These layers need to be removed in order to get to the fruit. This involves removing our emotional blockages and negative limiting beliefs.

I found spiritual knowledge and wisdom was also available to me through the literature of other spiritual traditions. There is a wealth of information in books published by people of all faiths, and of course online. I discovered that Kabbalah's truths are reflected in the teachings of other spiritual wisdom because spiritual truths are in fact universal. Whilst the way they are expressed may be packaged differently, the concepts they are all trying to express are one and the same.

We are Immortal, Eternal Souls

*You are an infinite spiritual being having
a temporary human experience.*
-Wayne Dyer

I had never thought too much about souls or the afterlife before my awakening. Yet now I had a deep knowing within that we are all eternal beings who have lived several lifetimes. I started reading about souls and what I discovered resonated greatly with me. I began to feel more connected to this inner part of myself.

My awakening had enabled me to truly experience, recognise and remember that we are all souls, infinite spiritual beings having a temporary human experience. The soul is the part of us that never dies. It is the part of us that is a part of God. The Talmud explains that before we are born an angel taps us on the upper lip making us forget what this world is about and who we truly are. But we can awaken to it.

We can remember that who we truly are is a soul, not this body and personality. When we die we return to being our true self, a soul without this body and character.

Connecting with our soul is connecting with God, as our soul is the God spark within us. It amazes me to think that we are each a tiny spark of God, of the Source. And that our souls are all connected, as we are all part of the One, the one God consciousness.

I never used to understand the term "Namaste" used in yoga. It is often translated as, "the God in me sees the God in you". I finally understood what it meant. It recognises that my soul is a part of God. My soul can see past your external personality and physical body and see through to your pure soul, your God spark, the God part of you.

I now understand that our soul spends a lifetime pulling at us to recognise and remember it, in order that we should align with it. Aligning with our soul is being true to our authentic selves, to our Divine essence. This is in contrast to identifying with our ego personality that is a construct comprising our experiences, influences, conditioning and limiting beliefs. When we are not aligned with our soul it brings conflict into our life, because it means not living the the the truth of who we are, why we are here and what we have come to do.

What does God really want from us? He wants us to connect to Him. To connect to the part of us that is Him, our soul. We can only do that by becoming our true selves. The problem is that we have been so conditioned and influenced by everything and everyone around us that we often lose the ability to listen to that guidance, our intuition. As children we are constantly aware of what everyone else wants from us that we learn to shut out and ignore the true voice that we are meant to be listening to. Divine guidance is with us all the time. By listening to our intuition, our Divine guidance, we will be on our path to our best selves and reach our highest potential.

Soul Growth

"We don't grow when things are easy; we grow when we face challenges."
-Anonymous

I received a deep understanding that despite us each being a pure soul, our 'character' or 'personality' in this lifetime is flawed. Essentially, we are presented with experiences that serve as soul lessons, and each of us has a unique curriculum. Overcoming the challenges we face enables us to grow and evolve. However, if we fail to learn the lesson, we will continue to encounter similar situations and scenarios as learning opportunities.

It is believed that before we come into this physical body our soul chooses many of our experiences, relationships and even our parents, in order to help us learn the lessons we have come here for. Examples of soul lessons include things like surrender, self-worth, compassion, non-judgement, forgiveness, patience, love, and authenticity.

For someone who had lived most of my life in victim mode, this was a big mindset shift. I had never really thought that we are actually here to face challenges, grow, evolve and elevate our soul. I wanted a quiet, easy life. Apparently, life isn't meant to be easy and without challenges! Our soul has chosen to come here to face challenges and overcome them.

Everyone has a unique curriculum with different lessons

their soul needs to learn and things they are here to overcome and accomplish in this world. Every soul is on their own individual path and we are all at differing stages of our soul journey. We come here with varied learning experiences depending on our stage.

Polarity is an inevitable part of this world. There will always be contrast. One can't have light without dark or good without evil. Therefore, we come here to learn, grow, and evolve by experiencing these contrasts. Our life experiences often reflect the contrast or antonym of what we are here to learn. For example, one might have experiences of powerlessness, in order to overcome this challenge and move into a state of feeling powerful. With this knowledge and understanding, I recognised my own challenges as opportunities to grow and became aware of my life lessons. Some of these revolve around guilt, shame, patience, and self-love. These are themes that have repeated for most of my life.

During my awakening, I had a sense that we exist far beyond this lifetime, including many other lifetimes. I truly felt and knew that this life was not all there is. It seems that our soul reincarnates over many lifetimes and goes through several soul levels as one learns lessons, experiences, grows, and evolves.

Love Thyself

"If I am not for myself, who will be for me?"
-Rabbi Hillel

I used to dislike the biblical phrase "Love Thy Neighbour As Thyself". I didn't understand what it meant to love thy neighbour as thyself, when I utterly hated myself. The years of depression had shaped my worldview to such an extent that I simply couldn't understand how this quote made any sense. What kind of dismal place would the world be if I actually went out there and loved other people as much as I loved (ie hated) myself? So instead I spent many years focused on being kind and loving to others whilst having no regard for myself.

It was only after my awakening that I truly got it. I was forced into being true to myself, honouring myself and following my intuition - my true self. I now realise that loving thyself is the important bit. The prerequisite upon which all else rests. There is an underlying assumption in the quote that we love ourselves. And until we learn to love ourselves, we really can't fully love anyone else. We can't truly come into ourselves and our purpose and give to the world like we are intended to until we love ourselves. "Love Thyself" isn't overtly explained in the Bible. Perhaps it's supposed to be so obvious that it doesn't need to be spelled out. Yet in today's world, most of us are so oblivious to the concept of self-love that we don't even register what the verse is really saying.

Perhaps once, people knew instinctively that we need to love ourselves in order to properly love others, but today loving thyself seems like a selfish indulgence. I always thought that it was synonymous with selfishness which to me was the ultimate insult. People who seemed to care more about themselves than about others triggered me. I thought they were the worst kind of people and conceitedly congratulated myself for being nothing like them. Many of us instinctively balk at the concept of putting ourselves first. We grew up in a world that preaches looking out for oneself is selfish and detracts from the far more important job of serving others. How wrong I was. I began to realise that what I labeled as selfish - putting yourself first - is in fact a necessary step to tuning in with our true self, our soul.

I slowly began to see that it must work the other way around. First, we learn to completely love and accept ourselves both for our positive qualities and our imperfections, and only then can we start to love others. We commit to the hard work of learning to forgive and love ourselves, because when we don't, we are no good to anyone. First, we fix ourselves and then we fix the world. Put on our oxygen mask and then help others. Like the quote above, "If I am not for myself, who will be for me?"

I wondered why loving ourselves was so important? And what does it mean to love oneself? I realised that it means being in alignment with one's soul - the part of God that resides within us. Wow, surely aligning with our soul is the most spiritual thing we can do. It is connecting to the Divine within us. How can we ignore the call to be true to ourselves?

Yet I still struggled with this whole concept. I was so used to loathing myself and neglecting myself in favour of others. When I was at my lowest, I didn't even know what my true self was, let alone have the faintest idea how to connect to it. I didn't know what I wanted on a day to day basis, I just knew that I was very far from where I needed to be. And so, I started my journey of self-discovery where I would try to learn to love myself and align with my soul.

I would guess that most of us do not value and love ourselves as we should, and it can be a long arduous process to learn to. It takes much work to change negative thought patterns and beliefs.

I had a glimpse of how the Divine sees us and how we are meant to see ourselves and others, through eyes of unconditional love. How many of us can say that we truly, unconditionally love ourselves? That is our goal, because once we have learnt to love ourselves properly, we can begin to serve others from a place of complete acceptance of who we are in this world and what we have to give. The more we love ourselves, the more love we will have to give to others.

Removing the Mask: Authenticity

"Before you can find God, you must lose yourself."
-Baal Shem Tov

I learnt the hard way. Being untrue to ourselves, to our soul, makes us miserable. When we are out of alignment, we don't feel happy or peaceful. We feel a sense of unease. We don't realise that it is our soul pulling at us to come into alignment. We mask the pain with coping mechanisms - depression, addiction, alcohol, obsessive exercise, overworking, overstudying, food, caffeine, tobacco, sugar, drugs etc. Most of us will not realise when we are not being true to our authentic selves, but we will feel some kind of pain. Our soul is trying to nudge us out of our lethargy and push us towards discovering our authentic self. Mine certainly was. When we don't listen to the nudges and guidance of our soul the messages get louder. Eventually messages may come in the form of illness, accidents, or a wake-up call of some sort.

When the Divine, God, our soul, or spirit is trying to get our attention to come into our true self, it is worth listening to.

Discovering our soul, and revealing our authentic self, requires taking off the masks one has been wearing. Removing the mask is stripping away how everyone else expects us to be and discovering our true self and purpose in this world. It involves removing the conditioning from the many sources that have influenced and stopped us from becoming our true self, in alignment with our soul.

Removing the mask also means dropping our inhibitions and caring less about what others think. It is something we do naturally as children but as we grow older, we become more and more influenced and inhibited adding layers to how we feel we ought to behave.

Our parents, culture, peers, schooling, and society have decided the way things 'should' be and what is 'expected' from us. But we are all different with unique talents and abilities that God wants us to use for our higher purpose. Every person needs to listen to their own guidance and their truth. What your parents or society wants from you might not actually be what you are here for. What is important for one person is not important for another. We are all on a very different, individual, journey with unique gifts and purposes.

I spent my childhood and my life trying to be like everyone else. Even as a parent bringing up kids, I assumed that encouraging them to do the same thing as everyone else and being part of the social crowd was how to give them self-esteem and put them on the road to happiness. I now realise it is the opposite. The pressure to be like everyone else prevents you from tapping into who *you* are really meant to be and what *you* are meant to be doing.

Often the people who learn this the most easily are unfortunately those who have a difficult childhood - the misfits, the odd ones. Whatever they do, they simply can't fit in with the crowd and so they are forced to go inwards and tune in to what *they* really want. They discover what they enjoy, their passions and ultimately their highest path. By learning to love and embrace themselves they avoid spending years building masks to be like everyone else. Many others tend to do what everyone else is doing. This is often not where their heart is guiding them and only later in life do they get the yearning and opportunity to become their true authentic selves.

For me it was four decades before I began to know myself. I had spent all that time in constant internal conflict, battling between what I wanted and what I thought I ought to want. Years of not actually listening to my heart, left me not even knowing who I truly was and what made me happy in this world. In order to tune in to my true self, I began questioning every decision I made and every action I undertook. Is this what I truly wanted or was it what was expected from me? Finding the answers meant stripping away the masks I had been wearing for so long. It required listening to my inner voice and thinking from my heart, not my head. Doing this, I began to break down the barriers of conditioning revealing my true self. Slowly, I began to heal.

The Talmud tells a story of a Rabbi crying on his deathbed, concerned that at the gates of heaven he will be confronted by God. He realized that God was not going to be asking him why he hadn't been more like Moses or King David but that he would be asked, why weren't you more like yourself?

It has been documented that one of the main things people regret when dying is that they hadn't been truer to themselves. And people near the end of their life usually want to be surrounded by authentic genuine people, not people wearing masks. Authenticity is showing our true self, our soul. It is removing the ego personality and letting our soul shine through. It is a shame that so many people only realise the importance of this as they near the end of life.

Oneness

*"The test of faith is whether I can make space for
difference. Can I recognize God's image in someone who
is not in my image, whose language, faith, ideal, are
different from mine? If I cannot, then I have made God in
my image instead of allowing him to remake me in his."*
-Rabbi Lord Jonathan Sacks

Before my awakening I was pretty judgmental, of myself and of others. I was living in a world where everyone is categorised by weight, height, colour, religion, academic achievement, job, status, sexuality, social class, looks etc. Consciously or unconsciously I would put people into a hierarchy of what I would think was better or worse.

During my awakening, I genuinely had sensed that we are all the same. That we all come from the same, are going back to the same and that we are all connected. Part of the One. A sense of Oneness. The way I like to see it, is that each of us is like a finger on a hand, feeling separate from the other fingers. However, we are in fact all connected. We are all part of the hand. Our souls are a part of, and inextricably connected to, God. This feeling that I had of Oneness is the opposite of duality where we feel separate from each other, from everything and from God.

It is this feeling of separation that is tearing the world apart. The lack of recognition that we are all connected and part of God, the One. This understanding should encourage us to have compassion and forgiveness for all sentient beings.

I began to analyse whether I really treated everyone equally. Was I as kind and friendly to the dirty, odd-looking, drunk, homeless guy as I would be to a rich, successful, gorgeous person? In Judaism, we are requested to be like God. Unconditionally loving and compassionate to everyone. No one is different in God's eyes. What right do we have to treat anyone differently or think badly about anyone?

Once we fully recognise this feeling of Oneness, that we are all connected, we can understand the reason why we are meant to be good, kind people. To 'fix' ourselves. What Judaism calls Tikkun Atzmi. If we are all part of God, the One, then what we do to another we are actually doing to ourselves. When we judge someone else, we are judging ourselves. When we harm someone else, we are harming ourselves.

I had always placed a large importance on trying to be an honest, decent person. Much of Judaism is about the laws between man and man and fixing one's character traits. We attempt to emulate God by being compassionate, loving, non-judgmental, kind, and honest. Furthermore, in the weeks following my awakening, there were incidents when I clearly felt an immediate cause and effect to my negative behaviour. It was then that I realised that karma exists for bad words, thoughts, and deeds. That we need to ensure we keep our words, thoughts, and actions pure and positive in order to not get hit with the effect of our bad behaviour.

I now understand why and to what extent we are meant to show unconditional loving, non-judgmental kindness at all times. To love and share unconditionally, having the desire to give without any desire to receive in return. We have the ability to see others like the Divine sees us, with compassion, forgiveness and non-judgmental acceptance and to recognize that we are all One and connected.

The Two Voices in my Head

*"Spiritual practices help us move from
identifying with the ego to
identifying with the soul."*
- Ram Dass

Meditation enables us to witness and observe our thoughts without becoming attached to and immersed in them. It helps us to recognise that we are not our thoughts, to learn to watch them and determine where they are coming from.

What I discovered through meditation is what I like to call the two voices in my head. They sound the same. Both sound like my thoughts. However, they are different.

The first 'voice' is the hyperactive mind, or what Buddhism would call the monkey mind. The incessant and unnecessary chatter of self-doubt, indecision and problem solving. It is way louder than the other voice and will go on for much longer. It tries to tempt me away from anything worthwhile and give me all the reasons why I should hate myself and why I'm not good enough. One might refer to this voice as the ego, the evil inclination, or in Kabbalah, the Satan. This voice is there to sabotage me, to make my life difficult and to keep me off track and all the while it tries to block me from hearing from the other voice which is my true essence, my soul.

I hear this second voice as my intuition. It is the kind,

gentle voice in my head that knows exactly what is best for me, what my true, pure essence is and what I should be doing. In fact, this voice is my true self, my heart, my soul, the God spark in me, my higher self. It is the part of me that resides in the eternal spiritual realm, that knows everything about me and what I am here for. This is the voice that wants to help me on my life journey and lead me to my highest potential. These are the positive, inspirational thoughts that I occasionally get during moments of clarity whilst in a place of calm like in the shower, meditating or out for a walk in nature. They are often the first thought that pops into my head when I think of a question, although they are often quickly followed by the ego which tries to talk me out of that thought, decision or idea.

Everyone is born with intuition and children know instinctively how to listen to it. However, despite always being present, through years of conditioning, and being told what to do and think, we suppress it to the extent that we no longer trust it or barely even hear it.

Meditation has taught me to take a step back from my thoughts, viewing them from an outside perspective in order to discern what type of thought is coming through. Is it the ego trying to keep me off track, or is it a pearl of wisdom coming through my intuition, my soul, with inspirational advice of what action or decision to take?

It took a long time for me to eventually be able to see my irrational, self-berating thoughts for what they were. But with persistence, I had amazing results. I am now often able to avoid getting caught up in a spiral of negative thinking. I can see my damaging, negative thoughts for what they are and know that they are just my ego trying to keep me off track. I tell them to go away and that I am not getting caught up in them. We can't choose what thought initially pops into our heads, but it is our decision whether to follow that thought with another one and another one and to let them spiral out of control.

Recognising our intuitive thoughts is one of our guidance systems. Often our intuitive guidance also comes through as feelings in our body. Intuition is often referred to as thinking with one's heart because we need to drop out of the angst in our head and into our body to know what we truly deeply really want. And the heart is where our soul resides. We also use the phrase 'gut feeling' to express that inner knowing in our gut that something is right or wrong. This is an example of feeling our intuition viscerally. Our body knows and tells us what it wants, although it takes time to recognise and master. When something doesn't feel right to me, I can feel a constriction in my stomach or chest. In contrast when something feels exactly on track, I may become aware of subtle, expansive, and relaxing feelings in my heart area. An intuitive guidance system is what Marie Kondo uses in her KonMari tidying, decluttering method! That is, checking whether each item 'sparks joy' and should be kept.

I spent four decades ignoring my intuition to the point I could barely hear it. Decision making was impossible. Everything needed to be rationalised. I was an analytical left brained thinker. I thought that logically analysing everything to death was the best way to be, and the sensible way to make decisions. Meditation was the one thing that helped to quieten down this ego voice and allow me to hear my intuition.

It is said that our mind can be our best friend or our worst enemy, but we need to be aware and choose which voice to listen to. Everything becomes reassuringly clear when we learn to listen to and follow our intuition.

Especially once we acknowledge that it is our guidance from our higher self that resides in the spiritual realm. This Divine guidance is constantly guiding us to our highest possibility, the most soul growth, and the next best step. Learning to ask for, access, receive and trust this Divine guidance takes work. Although our intuition is our sixth sense, it isn't just for mystics, or psychics. It is our direct connection to the Divine and available for everyone to access.

Ego: Standing in the Way of our Truth

"The problem is that we have allowed our egos, the part of us which believes that we are separate from God and separate from each other, to dominate our lives."
- Wayne Dyer

We can understand our ego as the *role* we are playing in this world rather than our true self. It is our personality or the character we have taken on. It is the labels we give ourselves, the mask that we wear and the image we have of ourselves.

Having an ego is human; all of us are born with one. The end goal and our challenge is to reach a state of enlightenment where we are able to transcend it; moving from our ego to our soul (higher self).

Our ego manifests as our desire to receive. Everything we do is because we want to get something in return, whether it be recognition, reward, self-esteem, or feeling loved. Overcoming our ego is achieved as our desire to create and give is stronger than it is to receive.

The process begins when we recognise that everything is from, and part of God and that we are all the same. Through meditation and prayer, we can nullify our ego recognising that nothing we have or have done is our doing, because everything comes from the Divine.

Our ego keeps us in our negative thoughts, ruminating. It has us consumed by our negative emotions, fears, and self-criticism. It needs validation from outside of ourselves and places our self-worth on these external things like looks, wealth, success, recognition, relationships etc. Our ego is part of being human. We can't get rid of it fully, but we can become aware of its presence and choose when to listen to it.

The world we currently live in 'feeds' our ego, by making us feel that looks, success, money and talent are the measures of a good life well led. However, it diverts and distracts us from the ultimate truth that living from our soul is how we know our true worth as an infinite spiritual being.

Consciousness & our Perception of the World

"I believe with perfect faith that the Creator, blessed be his name, is not a body, and that he is free from all accidents of matter, and that he has not any form whatsoever."
-Maimonides

My awakening was like a veil had been lifted off the world and I got a brief look behind the scenes. Spiritual experiences need to be experienced, not just studied, which is why meditation is a spiritual practice. It allows an expanded state of consciousness which leads to extra sensory perception. Regular, consistent meditation causes shifts in consciousness.

Soon after my awakening, I started reading a book about souls and what happens after death and between lives. Whilst reading, my entire body went into pure relaxation and resonance. My breathing went very slow, heavy, and deep. I somehow felt like I had come home. I felt like everything I was reading I already knew, and I was remembering where I came from. Somewhere deep down my soul was connecting to what I was reading, and it resonated with me at a soul level. I felt my consciousness expand as I read.

In fact, just taking in spiritual wisdom and letting it resonate at a deeper level can have profound effects. People may have shifts in consciousness by reading spiritual wisdom, such as the Zohar, The Power of Now, or The Secret. This can happen from listening to spiritual wisdom too, such as learning about the Three Principles. Knowledge that truly resonates with us at a soul level can cause expansions in consciousness. Furthermore, people have reported shifts in their consciousness from simply being in the company of an enlightened person whether it be Eckhart Tolle or the Lubavitcher Rebbe.

However, spiritual ideas cannot be understood intellectually. Each person will appreciate them at their own unique soul level and this wisdom has infinite levels of understanding. When it comes to spiritual wisdom, I can read a book, and then a few months later reread it understanding it in a totally different way. This knowledge is available for everyone, but it will meet them where they are at that moment.

Growing spiritually is expanding one's awareness and elevating to higher levels of consciousness. This is the way the Divine can flow directly through us and be received without interference from our ego, thoughts, and blockages. It is in this state that intuitive guidance, Divine inspiration, and messages are received more clearly. Many of the greatest artists, thinkers, writers, and musicians produced inspirational material that was channelled through them. This is what is referred to as being in a state of 'flow' or 'in the zone'. Inspiration means 'from spirit' or 'in spirit'. They are the vessel through which they can receive Divine inspiration from the spiritual realm. This doesn't come from the thinking ego mind. It comes directly from the part of us that is in the spiritual realm that is able to channel through us our highest and best potential.

Everything is Energy

*If you want to find the secrets of the universe, think
in terms of energy, frequency and vibration.*
-Nikola Tesla

I mentioned that a blockage in my energy centres had
been cleared and was responsible for my major shift in
consciousness but what did that actually mean? Everywhere
I looked there seemed to be modalities revolving around
energy that we can't see or feel. Reiki, feng shui, acupuncture,
tai chi, chi gong, EFT. Shamefully, I had written them all off
as nonsense, but it appeared that I needed to stop being so
cynical.

I slowly began to understand the concept that everything
in this world is made of energy that vibrates at a particular
level, a frequency. This includes people and objects as well as
thoughts, words, and emotions.

For example, emotions have their own frequencies, high
or low vibrational, depending on whether they are positive
or negative emotions. That is, whether they are coming from
Love or from *Fear*. Our thoughts create our emotions. Negative
thoughts lower our frequency and this in turn causes emotional
and physical distress. When we are vibrating at a low frequency
we feel bad and when we are vibrating at a high frequency we
feel good. Different things affect what level or frequency we are
vibrating at. Clearly my vibrational level had done a huge shift.

Emotions are energy in motion. They are intended to flow through us. However, when we don't process our emotions properly, they get stuck and blocked. These energetic emotional blockages and limiting beliefs, whether from trauma, conditioning or past experiences can get trapped in our energy centres and cause suffering and disease. These energy centres are known as Chakras in Buddhist and Hindu traditions and relate to the Sefirot in Kabbalah. They each correspond with and represent various aspects of our lives such as survival, stability, connection to the material world, creativity, sexuality, abundance, power, self-worth, courage, love, compassion, kindness, communication, expression, intuition and wisdom. Blockages in these centres prevent energy flowing through us. This energy is the Divine light that flows through our beings. Clearing our blockages is necessary in order to allow that Divine energy to flow through us and to raise our frequency.

The spiritual realm is a different dimension, vibrating at a much higher frequency. This physical Earth is much denser energy and once we die and lose our physical bodies we continue to exist as spirits, energetic beings, vibrating at a higher frequency. We lose our denser lower vibrational body and become a higher vibrational being, a spirit. Accessing the higher realms whilst in our physical body involves raising our vibration to match that realm.

God, the Infinite Light, is the source of this infinite energy streaming through the world. I now understand why people refer to God as Source, Oneness or Love. This energy is one of pure, unconditional love. I had experienced it for myself. There is a Divine presence in everything. Divine energy flows into everything.

Vibrations & Consciousness

*"The number one key to success in life is to master
your own state. If you can manage and master
your states, there's nothing you can't do."*
-Tony Robbins

I t appeared to me that the higher our vibration and the more
expanded our consciousness, the more aligned we are with
our soul and with the Source, God.

I made the connection that my awakening had caused my
vibrational frequency to be raised. I had also clearly experienced
an expansion of consciousness and wanted to understand the
connection between the two. I came across a diagram of David
Hawkins' Levels of Consciousness. It showed positive, *love*-
based emotions such as peace, joy and love being high vibrational
expanded states, while negative, *fear*-based emotions such as
guilt, shame, and fear were low vibrational and contracted states.
Enlightenment is the highest vibrational frequency followed
in descending order by peace, joy, love, reason, acceptance,
willingness, neutrality, courage, pride, anger, desire, fear, grief,
apathy, guilt and the lowest vibrational frequency being shame.
My awakening had given me a glimpse of that highest feeling
and I knew that was where we are meant to aim for.

As always, I wondered where all of this appeared within
Judaism. I then thought of some of the laws, phrases, and
traditions. How we are encouraged or commanded to be joyful,

to pursue peace, to love others and ourselves and to live from a place of faith, not fear. All of this seemed to be in alignment with what I was learning about vibrational states.

Whilst I had a sneaky peek at what enlightenment might look like, it became clear that it takes much work to reach and maintain a high vibrational state and expanded consciousness. In the period after my awakening I noticed that when I was off track, and let myself fall into negativity, the feelings of expanded consciousness diminished. I knew that working on raising my vibration and expanding my consciousness was the way to try to get back the amazing feeling I experienced during my awakening.

Gratitude holds a very high vibrational frequency and is used as a part of prayer within many traditions and within personal development and coaching. Gratitude journals have been shown to improve wellbeing. Staying in a state of gratitude is clearly being in a high vibration and expressing gratitude brings more things to be grateful for into our life.

I investigated what raises one's vibration. It seems so obvious now. All the things that society and science deem as healthy and good for one's well-being raise our vibration. Things like eating natural raw foods, ideally organic and unprocessed, meditating, music, exercise, being in nature, affirmations, positive thinking, gratitude, practising compassion, kindness, and forgiveness.

These ideas about raising our vibration and expanding our consciousness as we progress spiritually confirmed to me several things that religions already knew, and that science has also discovered are good for us. It appeared to me that everyone is trying to make sense of this world, work out what we are doing here and how to do it to the best of our ability. I believe religions are a guide to try to help us elevate spirituality and that science is trying to explain this world and much of what I believe mystics have known for years.

Thoughts Create Reality

"If you will it, it is no dream; and if
you do not will it, a dream it is
and a dream it will stay."
-Theodor Herzl

T he period after my awakening gave me a strong sense that I had the ability to control things with my mind. That my thoughts create my reality. I would have laughed at the absurdity of the concept had I not had a sense of it happening for me. As I began to experience and recognise it, I came across the Law of Attraction.

Assuming everything is vibrational energy, including our thoughts, the Law of Attraction claims that like energy attracts like energy. What we focus on we get more of. We attract into our life what we think about. As we choose happy feelings, more happy feelings will be drawn into vibrational harmony with the frequency we are offering. If we are constantly cranky and upset, then we will be inviting more of the same into our experience. It works like a big mirror. We create our vibrational frequency and send it out into the universe which draws to us, things, people, and experiences which are in alignment with our vibrational set point.

It took me a while to get my head around this stuff, that we attract positive things into our life by thinking positively. And that when we are vibrating at a high positive frequency, we attract more positive things into our life. Likewise, if we are thinking negatively, talking negatively, or acting negatively we will attract more negative experiences into our lives. Wow. I had been stuck in that negative rut in my life for many years. I had kept my depression going with my incessant negative thinking. I believed that. I had spent so many years wrapped up in my negativity, in a never-ending loop of limiting beliefs and thoughts that had kept me spiralling and experiencing more of the same.

I also knew that many experts in the field of Positive Psychology and Personal Development talk about how our mindset, PMA (positive mental attitude), positive self-talk and focus can determine our experience. And here it was, a spiritual concept in terms of energy saying the same thing. My CBT therapist and life coach had tried for years to get me to change my thought processes to more positive ways of thinking. I was a bit blown away. Is it really possible that our thoughts create our reality? I used to write off things like Positive Psychology and positive affirmations as mumbo jumbo.

Unsurprisingly, I had a hard time believing that our thoughts create our experience. However, after my awakening, I began to experientially feel it. I felt that I needed to be careful of how I focused my thoughts. I had always believed that my thoughts were just something private to me alone and now I was realising that our thoughts go out into the Universe, to the spiritual realm, and affect what happens in our life. How we think, speak and act all affects our reality. Meditation helped me become more aware of my thinking patterns. It taught me to observe my thoughts and recognise repetitive negative thinking loops into which I got myself.

It made me think of the concept that we are created in God's image. Is this what it meant? We are creators like God? That like God is a creator, we have also been made with the ability to create our lives, our experiences, and our reality.

I thought back to my Psychology degree where we learnt

about the concept of a Self-Fulfilling Prophecy. This refers to a belief or expectation that an individual holds about a future event that manifests because the individual holds it. A prediction that causes itself to be true due to the beliefs and behaviour of the believer. It made sense to me that we are able to create self-fulfilling prophecies with the law of attraction.

Another concept I had studied was Learned Helplessness. When people feel that they have no control over their situation, they may begin to behave in a helpless manner. This inaction can lead people to overlook opportunities for relief or change. I studied the learned helplessness theory of depression. Is that what I had experienced for almost two decades? Perhaps I was conditioned to believe that I couldn't escape my depression. And my negative beliefs kept me vibrating in that state, so that is what I was attracting into my life.

The most obvious example to me of the law of attraction was something we referred to regularly in Psychology, the Placebo Effect. When people experience a benefit after receiving a fake, sham treatment. A certain percentage of people would always have improved symptoms simply by taking a sugar pill. This phenomenon is always taken into account in psychology research studies. Is the placebo effect scientific proof that the law of attraction works I wondered? How thinking positively that something might help enables a positive response. Wow. This also made total sense to me and I wondered why we had spent so much time in psychology accounting for the placebo effect but never actually looking at why it was effective. In my studies it was written off as something that annoyingly affected statistical research results and needed to be considered. But we never investigated why the placebo effect worked. There is clearly a mind over matter connection.

I had always laughed with my husband. His headache would disappear as he took the painkillers out of the box before even swallowing them. His positive thinking and focus clearly helped him. He just needed to think about taking a painkiller and it working and his headache would disappear. In contrast, most painkillers and medicines didn't help me because truthfully, I never really believed they would. My pessimistic nature evidently affected their results on me too.

Our thoughts and our minds have the power to heal us. We do have the ability to create our reality and so I understood why positive psychology is so popular and why affirmations actually can work. I was in such a bad place beforehand that I could not even contemplate that positive focus could work. I now understand that our minds have the power to affect our lives, our emotions, our feelings, and our realities. That when we say something, feel it, believe it, visualise it, persevere and are grateful, we are truly able to bring amazing things into our lives. Visualisation is also a key component of the law of attraction. Athletes have known for years the power of visualisation techniques and how they can impact performance.

Prayer and intention can also be attributed to the law of attraction, in that thoughts and prayers are energy being sent out to the universe. So, focusing our thoughts on something we want can enable it to manifest. This would include how praying for someone is sending them positive healing energy.

I began to understand how our intentions create our reality. How our emotions, attitudes, thoughts, words and actions reflect our intentions. How we need to be mindful and aware of the intentions we project. And how we need our conscious and subconscious intentions to be positive or we end up like me in a two-decade depression. I realised that the soul growth we are here for is through overcoming negative thought patterns and emotions to create a different experience for ourselves. It can be quite a harsh, scary truth to accept that we have such control over our life and that to a certain extent we are responsible and do co-create our own reality.

The Power of Nature

"In a crystal we have clear evidence of the existence of a formative life principle, and though we cannot understand the life of a crystal, it is nonetheless a living being."
-Nikola Tesla

When pondering about vibrations, I remembered something about crystals and energy. I pulled out a jar of crystals I had bought years earlier. I had entertained my young child's fascination with them and gone to a crystal store near our home. In the store, each crystal had a list of its healing properties written on a note next to it. I didn't understand what it was all about. I scoffed my way around the store, rolling my eyes. They were just inanimate pretty stones in different colours. I had laughed at the ridiculousness that people thought these hard, inanimate rocks could do anything, let alone heal any of the ailments mentioned next to them. I had even asked the assistant in the store what was the deal with the crystals? She said the stones were high vibrational, whatever that supposedly meant....

So here I was, a couple of years later, and took myself back again to the crystal shop to try to take off my skeptic's hat and see if there might be something to it. If I now buy into this energy stuff, what might that mean regarding these stones? I started to put a crystal or two in my pocket and bought a couple for friends. I continued to be skeptical, but my friends all fell in love with the crystals, noticed changes and improvements in their lives and attributed it to the crystals!

The next time I went back to the shop a thought popped into my head. Perhaps God created this world in such a way that we have natural things like plants, herbs, flowers and crystals to help heal us, as opposed to God planning for thousands of years down the line we would invent and create little white round pills to help deal with all sorts of ailments. Okay, now *that* spoke to me. I thought of the dozens of medications I had taken that hadn't helped me and wondered whether we have gone so off the path from what God created and intended for those simple, natural things to aid in our healing.

I was still slightly skeptical though and wondered what if anything Judaism had to say about crystals. Quite a lot it turned out. I discovered that crystal properties are known within Judaism too. That the High Priest's breastplate was adorned with 12 different crystals for each of the 12 tribes and that they were believed to have had healing properties. And that there were also the crystals Urim and Thurim used for divination. It appeared that the powers of crystals had also been recognised in Jewish sources too. I just hadn't known it.

Kabbalah has always believed Amulets, stones, and gems to have magical powers. They were known to possess healing and spiritual powers. Amulets were believed to help achieve things like success in career, remove the evil eye, give protection, guidance, healing etc. When placed in your vicinity it is believed that these things can shift your energy field and create changes in different aspects of your life. I was amazed. Even my solid religion believed in this weird stuff. I felt like this cynic needed to begin eating her words.

As I continued to read about crystals, I discovered that one needs to cleanse them to keep their vibrations high and remove from them negative energy that they have absorbed. Sounded weird to me but I played along and bought a smudge stick of sage that is meant to do the job. Apparently, it also clears the energy in spaces and homes. It was so foreign to me and still felt a bit weird and wacky. Yet again, I wondered if all this stuff was true then where was it in Judaism?

A few weeks later, near a Rabbi's grave, I noticed a stall selling herbs and incense to burn to remove the 'evil eye'. I guess this is another way of saying to remove low negative vibrations. Once again, it seemed like these 'crazy' ideas were to be found in the religion of my upbringing. I could no longer dismiss any of this stuff. It was so far out of my comfort zone, but it was fascinating, and I was curious what else out there could shake me and my opinions up.

Emotions: Our Guidance System

*There can be no transforming of darkness into light
and of apathy into movement without emotion.*
-Carl Jung

The spiritual journey I had suddenly found myself on meant that I needed to start processing my emotions and healing. In the period of time after my awakening I was aware that I had got emotions all wrong. During that time, my emotions came and went like waves. They would flow through me in a very natural way and I had an inability to suppress them. Tears would come and, unlike the years before, I would have no choice but to let the emotion wash over me. And so, I realised that we are meant to fully feel our emotions and allow them to pass through us. The word emotion has its roots in Latin meaning energy in motion. To flow through us rather than meet resistance. When we resist, fight, or suppress our emotions, they get stuck in our energy system. These emotional blockages can then stay with us causing problems for years until we are ready to bring them up into our awareness, process, feel, and release them.

We all have emotional blockages to deal with. I used to think that 'trauma' meant that someone had suffered a severe traumatic experience. I now realise that everyone has 'trauma', it is our response to distressing events. Little incidents in infancy, childhood and throughout our lives that shape our beliefs and how we react to things. 'Traumas' could include when a teacher once called you lazy, causing years of you believing it. Or being left to cry for 3 minutes in your cot (crib) causing later abandonment issues within relationships. These 'traumas' cause self-limiting beliefs that hold us back in life, prevent us from healing and create emotional issues. If emotional issues aren't dealt with, physical problems can follow.

Our emotions and triggers are our guidance system. When we are triggered with a negative emotion it is often a reminder, a throwback to an incident - usually in our early childhood, when we experienced a trauma. Healing often involves going back and processing an emotion that had not been fully felt. During meditative work, traumas often resurface for us to process and then release. This doesn't always come with the awareness of what the trauma was, but it comes with a wave of emotion that we can allow to pass through our body. These old memories and traumas that have been stored in our system are then able to release themselves.

Our emotions come in response to our thoughts. And like our thoughts we can just allow them to come and go without getting caught up in them or resisting them. Allowing and acknowledging them rather than suppressing or denying them. Fully accepting and loving ourselves means fully accepting our emotions and allowing ourselves to properly feel them.

Fear vs Love

"There are two basic motivating forces: fear and love. When we are afraid, we pull back from life. When we are in love, we open to all that life has to offer with passion, excitement, and acceptance. We need to learn to love ourselves first, in all our glory and our imperfections. If we cannot love ourselves, we cannot fully open to our ability to love others or our potential to create. Evolution and all hopes for a better world rest in the fearlessness and open-hearted vision of people who embrace life."
-John Lennon

There was something very clear to me during my awakening. That the feeling and energy emanating from this huge light source, from the spiritual realm, was one of pure blissful unconditional love. It was beyond words. I felt such awe. Awe but with no fear involved. Just pure wonder, amazement, love, and reverence. I knew that the universal force, the light, the energy from the Creator was *love*. And I knew that being surrounded by this unconditional love is what it feels like to be in the spiritual realm, close to the Divine.

I quickly recognised that fear is not an emotion we are meant to be carrying around with us all the time. My severe anxiety that I had lived with for years disappeared during my awakening. Even afterwards, there were many things that I used to be anxious about that no longer affected me.

Our stress reaction, the fight or flight response, is our protective mechanism to prepare the body to react to danger. When being attacked by a wild animal, it protects our physical safety. I had been living in a permanent state of stress. In a constant state of high alert. I realised we are not designed to be living in a state of fear but in a state of bliss and unconditional love, like the energy of the Divine. Fear has its place for dangerous situations where physical safety is threatened but everyday stressing is keeping us and the world in the low vibrational frequency of fear.

I had gone from being very right wing to being very left wing overnight. I realised that my right-wing tendencies had come from a place of fear and from a feeling of separation, not of oneness, of what could happen, of war, of losing our country, etc. Those questions and arguments were still valid, but they all came from a place of fear, and I knew that fear is not what is going to lead to world peace, that the opposite is needed. I know that only love is going to change this world through the removal of the lower vibrations of anxiety, fear, and hate.

When we believe that we are different from each other, we live in a place of fear. Once we recognise that we are all connected, not separate, we can begin to live from love. There is a constant fear of death that is driving so many lives. This comes from a feeling of separation from the Divine, our source, our creator and from a lack of consciousness, that we are immortal souls, that live forever. When we truly, fully embrace this concept, we are much more likely to live fearlessly and to see a larger picture.

Unfortunately, I now know that this world and I were holding so much fear and that many parts of our lives and decisions are driven by fear. My clinical anxiety was gone but I was still left with many ingrained fear-based beliefs and work to do on clearing them.

The opposite of love is not hate. It is fear. People acting with hatred are doing so from a place of fear. All emotions stem from love or fear. All decisions can be made from a place of love or fear. From lower or higher vibrational emotions. I understood that living from our ego mind is fear-based and that living from our soul is based in love. I began to become aware of when I was thinking from my ego from a place of fear or when I was operating from my soul from a place of love. I wanted to be guided by my soul, not the fears of my ego mind.

Holding us Back:
Self-Limiting Beliefs

*"Man often becomes what he believes himself to be. If
I keep on saying to myself that I cannot do a certain
thing, it is possible that I may end by really becoming
incapable of doing it. On the contrary, if I have the
belief that I can do it, I shall surely acquire the capacity
to do it even if I may not have it at the beginning."*
-Mahatma Gandhi

S elf-limiting beliefs are assumptions, ideas and
perceptions that are usually negative and limit and
hinder our growth. They are often adopted in childhood
and are very difficult to change or shed. Many of them reside
in our subconscious.

Meditation allows us more conscious awareness of the self-
limiting beliefs that are holding us back in life. These beliefs
can prevent us from reaching our highest potential, living our
best life, and stepping into our soul's purpose. By beginning
to witness our thoughts and emotions we can observe these
damaging thoughts rather than getting immersed in them.
This, in turn, allows us to analyse them, perhaps discover
their root cause and may lead us to identify those beliefs as
invalid and distorted. We then have the possibility to reframe
or dismiss these self-limiting beliefs.

It was the Mindfulness course that my psychiatrist ran that first introduced me to the concept of limiting beliefs. However, life coaching and many psychological therapies also focus on identifying, changing, and clearing them.

Everyone has limiting or negative beliefs that can be worked on. Small events, traumas and our general upbringing conditions our childhood and influences our belief systems. So whether we grew up believing we should be seen and not heard, we couldn't trust others, we were not clever enough, lazy or ugly, these limiting beliefs can be removed in order for us to live our best life and fulfill our soul's purpose. Often these limiting beliefs stem back to a core subconscious belief that we hold about ourselves and this world.

Because we are so open and susceptible during our early childhood years, we take on beliefs from what we were told or experienced and carry them with us through life. When these beliefs are negative, they drag us down and prevent us from moving forward and fulfilling our potential. Recognising a limiting belief and then understanding that it is not serving us, is the first step. However, we are often so immersed in them that we can't even see that they are holding us back; we do not even realise that they might not be true. It's not crucial to actually know where our limiting beliefs stem from in order to work at clearing them. The important part is the awareness and the intention to release them.

Meditation practice and an understanding of this concept enabled me to recognise my negative thoughts and belief patterns and this awareness allowed me to identify those beliefs and to start to clear them. The spiritual path always involves removing our limiting beliefs and taking us back to our innocent unprogrammed, unconditioned, authentic self where Divine light and energy can flow easily through us.

We are all Mirrors:
Reflections & Triggers

*"Everything that irritates us about others can
lead us to an understanding of ourselves."*
-Carl Jung

After my awakening I began to have many vivid dreams. After one particularly gruesome 'nightmare', I saw an advertisement for a dream workshop to understand and interpret dreams. I was intrigued and needed to get to the bottom of the frightening dream I had encountered. The workshop was run by a psychotherapist. It became clear to me while discussing our dreams and the subconscious mind that our dreams are messages and guidance from the spiritual realm. That through understanding our dreams, which are usually presented in metaphors, we receive insights as to how we are doing on our soul's path and how to navigate life. It was fascinating.

During a guided visualisation that took place in the workshop, we were encouraged to visualise someone we disliked. I don't tend to really dislike people, but I decided to focus on someone who years earlier annoyed me. After the visualisation, we discussed how we are all a reflection of each other. People who trigger us, irritate us or who we dislike, are there reflecting to us our shadows, aspects of ourselves that we reject, are unhappy with and want to change. These are unconscious facets of us that need healing or integrating. I squirmed at first. I didn't believe it. The person I had thought of bothered me because she was attention seeking, super confident and seemed to overly love herself. I didn't want to be like that and hence she annoyed me. As far as I was concerned, they were not good character traits and I rejected the notion that I should or would want to be more like her. I thought I wanted to be the exact opposite.

On reflection however, I understood the truth of it and realised it was right. She triggered me because she had those qualities that I lacked. I did actually need to love myself more, be more confident and be more willing to be seen, even though my ego would try to convince me otherwise. These were rejected aspects of myself that I could recognise and integrate.

It's humbling to admit that I was often irritated by people who to me seemed selfish and to look after their own needs first (like I mentioned in the chapter about loving thyself). I finally understood that it was because it was something I needed to work at. I needed to love myself more.

As my awareness expanded, I became aware of triggers surrounding me in every interaction and relationship. Whenever someone or some interaction would bother me, I would assess what I disliked about it or them. I then tried to figure out what that reflected about myself and which aspects I needed to address and heal. These wounds that required healing often stemmed from childhood experiences and limiting beliefs that came from decades earlier.

I was forced to look at my shadows, the unconscious aspects of my personality, the wounds and fears that I choose to hide as I deem them 'ugly'. These parts that still often drive my thoughts, feelings and behaviour.

Every relationship we have and everyone we meet is our

mirror. The outside world we perceive, and our relationships, are a reflection of our inner world. Our inner reality is reflected back to us. We judge and criticise others because we are actually judging and criticising ourselves. Negative responses and triggers about someone/something show us that there is something there to be resolved, something unexpressed or unintegrated within ourselves. Others can reflect back to us positive aspects that we can integrate or negative traits for us to overcome. They show us the things we don't like about ourselves, and the things we need more of in order to teach us to love, accept and forgive ourselves fully. Positive responses, when we are triggered by others in a good way, are a reflection of something that we already have or desire.

How we feel on the inside is reflected back to us as we are manifesting our realities from our feelings. As within, so without. Someone who is angry on the inside will experience more people who, and situations that, reflect back to them anger, and give them experiences where they feel anger.

Triggers set off in me a reminder of a belief I hold. I therefore use it as an opportunity to see what lesson there is for me to learn and what aspect of me requires healing or integrating. For example, if someone lets me down and it makes me upset or angry, I recognise that it is bringing up my long-standing belief that I can't rely on others.

The first step to change and heal an aspect of ourselves is the awareness and acceptance of it. It is because of these reflections and triggers that our relationships in life are our biggest challenges and are also our biggest opportunities and areas for soul growth.

The Journey is Tough

"The entire purpose of our existence is
to overcome our negative habits"
-Vilna Gaon

I hope no one has read this far and thought that my life changed overnight, and I lived in the land of fairies and roses from thereon. As I explained, I only had a glimpse of enlightenment, a peek of what we could be aiming for, of where we could be heading. Then began the hard work and process of aligning with my true self and healing my emotional blockages. This involves uncovering traumas, discovering limiting beliefs and working on thoughts and emotions to release fears and to start to live a meaningful, authentic life, true to my soul's path. Those days in that state of bliss were an incredible gift. Now I knew what was possible and there was no going back, it was time to forge ahead.

The first step was to start loving myself. This was key and as it is for many people, it's an ongoing process. To fully love and accept oneself is a lifetime of work, especially if you spent four decades truly hating yourself. This includes constantly tapping in with my intuition and following the desires of my soul, my true self and not my ego. This isn't an easy feat considering the conditioning most of us have and the stigma surrounding looking after oneself first.

I now had a sharper awareness of what had been holding me back, causing my fears and making me miserable. Being able to observe my thoughts rather than getting caught up in them allowed me to see which thoughts kept coming up causing angst and negative emotions within me. These thoughts were usually able to be tracked back to limiting beliefs that I held about myself and my life. Sometimes these beliefs were deep in my subconscious, from a trauma, or from years of conditioning and identifying with that belief.

Recognising these beliefs and seeing them for what they were, (repeated thinking patterns that were on loop in my mind, from past conditioning or trauma) allowed me to begin to let them go. It takes much hard work to change deeply ingrained negative thinking patterns. Years of coaching and therapies had tried to work on them but with few results. Thanks to meditation, I now had much more of an ability to observe my cognitions and therefore work on my thoughts, and release or adjust them.

My emotions also became a tool that I used to guide me. I learned to become aware when I was experiencing a negative emotion, recognise its cause and see what aspect of myself needed to be healed.

As one's awareness expands, the unconscious becomes conscious. This means that even traumas that are repressed can come up to be processed and healed. I added deep inner child and shadow work to identify and heal some of the painful, hidden wounds I was holding. These blockages prevent the light from flowing through us and in order to elevate spiritually they need to be removed.

Psychological healing overlaps with spiritual growth. This personal healing is a necessary part of the spiritual path for us to evolve. This process is so unique and individual as each of us has different aspects to heal and different limiting beliefs and emotional blockages holding us back. Through this inner healing work, I found many physical ailments resolved themselves too. Emotional blockages are stuck energy which can cause mental and physical disease. It is through inner work that people have been able to miraculously heal themselves of major physical illnesses.

The Art of Surrender

*"Surrender is the simple but profound
wisdom of yielding to rather than
opposing the flow of life."*
- Eckhart Tolle

An important aspect of the spiritual path is learning the art of surrender. Resisting against our pain only perpetuates it. As psychologist Carl Jung said, "what you resist, persists". This is where struggle and suffering occur. It is said that pain is unavoidable, but suffering is a choice. We can learn to surrender to our pain and our emotions in order to allow them to flow through us and not leave trauma and blockages behind. I believe we are challenged to let go of a victim mentality by learning to surrender to circumstances beyond our control. We do this by recognising that everything supposedly negative that is happening is not happening *to* us or *against* us but is in fact, happening *for* us. There is a bigger picture at hand, and we can trust it.

I spent most of my life in victim mode. 'Poor me' syndrome. I thought that I needed to avoid pain at all costs and resisted it whenever possible. I now realise that we aren't here to sail through life having an easy time. We are here to grow, evolve and expand and that happens through lessons and challenges. Difficult things occur to assist in our expansion and evolution.

We can overcome them, learn from them, and grow, change and blossom from the challenges.

It isn't usually easy to remember these things in the middle of difficult times. So often we look at our challenges and say, "Why me? Where is God? How could God allow this to happen?" It takes an expanded perspective to be able to see what everything is really about. A perspective that we don't fully have whilst living as humans on this Earth. Only once we die and return to being spirits do we fully understand how every little thing we went through was all part of the Divine plan for us to help our souls grow, learn and experience. It has been taught that our soul also chooses some of the lessons, experiences, and challenges it will face in this lifetime before it descends down to Earth.

During tough times it is difficult to take this zoomed out perspective when all we want is to get ourselves out of pain rather than surrender to it. We simply cannot see the big picture, nor how it could be helping us. In these moments, it is best to remain in a place of faith and trust that everything is happening for our greater good. Knowing that one day we'll understand it all and be glad we surrendered.

Surrender does not mean giving up. It means standing in a place of humility and recognising our limitations. It isn't easy. It requires conscious effort. It means challenging our thoughts and beliefs and releasing attachment to outcomes, trusting that we shall be given exactly what we need, not what we think we need. When we release our need to control situations, people, goals, and outcomes, we surrender and open ourselves up to the Divine, knowing that we are supported and loved more than we can possibly imagine.

Mind-Body Connection

*"Illnesses do not come upon us out of the
blue. They are developed from small daily
sins against Nature. When enough sins have
accumulated, illnesses will suddenly appear."*
-Hippocrates

I never used to believe in the mind-body connection, despite my husband having had the original and primary mind-body disease: a stomach ulcer. It has been known by doctors since the mid-twentieth century that peptic ulcers are indeed caused by suppressed stress. That did sum up my husband. He didn't show his emotions or stress. They were buried deep in his ulcer. Although that connection was accepted by modern medicine, and I could see it firsthand, I was still a skeptic. I myself had numerous ailments with inexplicable causes and which didn't respond properly to treatment. Even prior to my awakening I had begun to notice the mind-body connection with regard to chronic headaches that I regularly suffered with. I remember sitting with friends and the conversation would stress me out. Something daft and random, like how everyone else had bought and organised their kids school books for the next year. As I became aware of the stress I was feeling, I could feel a headache creeping up my neck to my head. I knew I got stress headaches but had never felt it so obviously and immediately.

Conventional medicine and science have long ago acknowledged the effect stress can have on the physical body. I attended a workshop about the mind-body connection and how each part of our body is connected to different emotions and issues, and, true enough I became aware when my body would indicate something going on with me emotionally. I then started to observe those around me and the ailments they would suffer with when they clearly had a lot of emotional stuff going on in their life. I would think of my health issues and how modern medicine had never properly helped with any of them. There was evidently more going on, and it appeared to me that stress might not be the only emotional cause of physical issues.

Following my awakening, several of my physical ailments cleared up by themselves. As well as the depression and anxiety which suddenly disappeared, my migraines improved, and my chronic constipation went away. I became aware that we have a far greater ability to heal ourselves than I ever thought was possible and there is likely an emotional component to every physical ailment.

Accepting this reality, however, brings much discomfort as it requires us to look inwards. It demands that we stop blaming external causes for our illnesses and instead do the inner emotional, psychological, and spiritual work to bring about true healing.

The consequences of an over reliance on western medicine and pharmaceuticals are that we fail to appreciate the amazing way we have been created and the power we have to heal ourselves. The truth is, as more research is done, the more the mind-body connection is recognised as scientific fact and that ancient or non-conventional healing modalities have a strong base in science too.

I am of the opinion that illness is the soul's way of communicating the need for change. It is telling us that there is emotional healing to be done. Whilst I believe that there is a place for modern medicine, I also hold that physical ailments have emotional and spiritual causes. I believe that we often have the ability to heal ourselves through inner work together with natural treatments that have been available and used for thousands of years.

The Present Moment

"Realize deeply that the present moment is all you ever have. Make the NOW the primary focus of your life."
-Eckhart Tolle

'd spent most of my life as far from the present moment as is humanly possible. In fact, I barely knew what it meant. That is what depression and anxiety do. They keep you constantly in your thoughts, ruminating about the past or stressing about the future and never actually living in the present.

People say, 'Enjoy every moment!'. That concept was so alien to me. I even remember on my wedding day feeling so distant, that I was telling people I couldn't wait to watch the video because it felt like I wasn't really there. Enjoying any moment isn't really an option when you are so out of your body and caught up in your thoughts.

Pure bliss is found in the present moment. My awakening took me fully into the present. When we think of something that felt absolutely joyful it is usually because it pulled us into the present moment. Experiences like breathtaking scenery, adrenaline inducing sporting activities and being in nature, all force us out of our thinking and into enjoying the here and now.

Meditative activities are all about focusing on the present moment. This doesn't just mean a silent sitting meditation but includes things like exercise, dance, arts & crafts, cooking or walking. Mindfulness teaches us to get out of our thoughts and into the now moment by doing things mindfully and focusing on our 5 senses. The guided walking meditation I referred to earlier taught me how to concentrate on all my senses, by becoming aware of everything as if observing it for the first time. Sometimes after practising it, my senses would heighten so much that colours, textures and shapes would pop out into a vivid, sharper visual experience.

During my awakening, I felt extremely present. I wasn't thinking at all about the past or the future. I wasn't even able to stress! Despite how challenging it is to remain in it, I realised that the ideal state to be in is fully present in the now. The present moment is all we have. The past has gone, the future may never happen, so the present is the only thing we truly have.

A Relationship with the Divine: Prayer & Connection

"Be still and know I am God."
-Psalms 46:10 (11)

Before my awakening I had never truly connected to the Divine through prayer. I would say the words in Hebrew, sometimes understanding them, but usually not, and that would be my prayer. I was definitely not in any sort of meditative state when praying. I didn't know that a deeper, better connection was possible.

Through meditation and my awakening, I became aware that through our breath we can access the Divine realm. Our breath is the bridge between this physical realm and the spiritual realm. When we focus on it, we can use our breath and the stillness of meditation to expand our consciousness and access beyond the veil. This means connecting with the Divine for connection, for prayer and for guidance. Clarity comes when we focus on our breath and still our mind. This clarity is our intuition, our soul, our higher self, the part of God within us that resides in the spiritual realm channeling inspiration and Divine guidance through us.

I now understand why it is said that prayer is when you talk to God and meditation is when you listen to God. From a higher vibrational frequency, we are closer to that realm and our prayers and intentions are more easily heard and answered.

Before starting meditating, I had so many preconceptions about meditation. What is it? What isn't it? Who is it for? Who isn't it for? I approached meditation as a totally non-spiritual practice - purely from scientific research giving proven statistical evidence that it is effective in reducing anxiety and depression.

When I first started meditating, I would find that online it was often referred to as a spiritual practice. I didn't understand what they meant. The MBSR Mindfulness course taught meditation and its benefits from a purely medical, scientific perspective and didn't recognise it as a spiritual practice at all. It was through my awakening that I realised that meditation is the portal to the spiritual.

I began to wonder why the Judaism I had been practising didn't include meditation in the prayer services since it is evidently such an effective way to connect directly to the Divine. Through more research, I discovered that meditation was a huge part of Jewish prayer way back in Biblical times and it is often referred to in the Bible. And meditative practices are included in Jewish mysticism, Kabbalah, Hasidism, Mussar and more. Apparently, prayer in mainstream Judaism used to include meditation but it faded from use leaving a rigid and fixed form of prayer.

Unless one knows the words by heart like a mantra and is able to close their eyes while praying, I imagine it is very difficult if not impossible to get fully into a meditative state through the formal Jewish prayers that many people use nowadays. What my awakening made me realise is that meditation is the ultimate spiritual practice. It is the tool to connect to the higher realms, to the larger part of this world that we don't get to see and experience.

After persisting with it for a length of time, with discipline and consistency, meditation connects us with, and enables access to, the higher realms. And once we are in these higher realms, our communication has much more power. Having a prayer, thought or intention during meditation is a direct line of communication with the Divine.

Through meditation we can receive Divine guidance. Our guidance can come in many forms but its most basic is our intuition. Everyone is born with intuition but often throughout our years it becomes shut down. Meditation can bring it back and heighten it. Through the calmness of meditation, we quieten the other voices and thoughts in our head and more clearly get guidance, inspiration, and answers, through our intuition, our soul. It was very exciting and powerful for me to fully acknowledge that our intuition is our guidance from the Divine. I wondered how I could ever not follow my intuition once knowing this.

It was through meditation that I learnt to pray with real intention. The Hebrew word for intention, kavana, is used in Judaism all the time. I used to think it meant directing your concentration on the words and not letting your mind wander. However, I never really understood the words I was saying, so although my attention was on the words, my intention never was. I never actually set an intention. Now I realise that it is important to understand the words when praying and to mean them. To have true focused intent. We choose our intention and our focus, and it is these that shape our reality. This is part of the law of attraction. Negative emotions reflect negative intentions which creates negative results in our reality. Our prayers should include conscious intentions. Because in fact, we are constantly sending out prayers and intentions - whether consciously or unconsciously.

Every intention which is a thought, word or action has a

cause and its effect. We are responsible for the effect of every intention we have. What we put in is what we get back. Having an intention during prayer or meditation is the way to fulfill our desires and bring our dreams, hopes and prayers into reality.

The mystics who have been known to cause magical healings and miracles are in an elevated state, closer to the spiritual realm and are more easily able to tap into that realm and set an intention for something and then receive it. It is another form of prayer and it is often through meditation practice that they have these special gifts.

As I had felt, our physical world is only a tiny fraction of what really goes on. There is so much more that we cannot perceive with our five senses. However, that other spiritual realm - that we often don't talk about (well I never did) is very real. It encompasses souls, angels, God and all sorts of higher beings that are so difficult for us to grasp conceptually. It is through meditation that we can have access to the extra sense needed to gain knowledge and to experience this realm.

Receiving Divine Guidance & Signs

"The world is full of wonders and miracles but man takes his little hand and covers his eyes and sees nothing."
-Baal Shem Tov

The following story is one that I was told as a child and have heard numerous times since. You may have heard it too but bear with me.

The story is of a man, who was a firm believer in God. One day it began to rain very heavily. It kept raining and a big flood came. The man climbed up on the roof of his house and knew that he would be ok. God would protect him. It kept raining and now the water had reached his waist.

A boat came by and a guy in the boat said: "Hey, jump in. We will take you with us". "No, thanks," said the man. "I'm a firm believer in God. He will rescue me." He sent the boat away. It kept on raining and now the water had reached his neck. Another boat came by and a guy in the boat said: "You look like you need some help. Jump in and we shall take you with us". "No," said the man. "I'm a firm believer in God. He will rescue me. Don't worry about me". The boat sailed away. It still rained and the water now reached his mouth. A helicopter came by and a guy in the helicopter threw down a rope and said: "Hi there, my friend. Climb up. We shall rescue you." "No," said the man. "I'm a firm believer in God. He will rescue me. I know He will." The helicopter flew away.

It kept on raining, and finally the man drowned. When the man died, he went to heaven. When entering heaven, he had an interview with God. After giving a polite greeting, the man asked: "Where were you? I waited and waited. I was sure you would rescue me, as I have been a firm believer all my life and have only done good to others. So where were you when I needed you?" God scratched his confused looking face and answered: "I don't get it either. I sent you two boats and a helicopter."

I used to think the story meant that we are obligated to help ourselves and not just to expect God to save us. But now since experiencing the feeling of Divine guidance I realise that we often miss our guidance. Perhaps that is the key to the story. God probably isn't going to send some supernatural miracle or big event to help us. God hides behind nature, behind everything natural and normal. So, we should look out for the very subtle signs of help and guidance we are sent. We can get in tune with them, recognise them and grab them. The Divine isn't hidden from us, it is just guiding us in a very subtle way. What we often think of as coincidences aren't by chance. In fact, I believe there is no such thing as a coincidence.

After my awakening, my senses opened up to how the Divine is available to us, sending us signs, symbols and messages. Messages and guidance surround us in forms we never would have normally considered coming from a Divine source. Synchronicities, dreams, animals, repeating numbers, music, ailments, intuitions, chance meetings and messages in things we hear, read, or come across. Weird. Yup. But also beautifully amazing.

Synchronicities begin to occur as the veil thins between the physical and the spiritual realm. Carl Jung coined the term synchronicity to mean a meaningful coincidence. When they happen, one often realises that it wasn't just a random coincidence and there is more going on in the world that we can perceive.

It is said that our angels never sleep, they are always with us. And we are able to communicate with them and receive their guidance. They are expressions of the Divine, carrying out acts of God.

Like with the law of attraction, it requires belief. If we don't believe it can happen, we won't experience it. However, we can ask for guidance, believe it, raise our vibration, expand our consciousness, and then look out for the magic.

With an expanded awareness and perspective, we can see that there is a spiritual meaning behind virtually everything, and that normal occurrences or coincidences are often actually signs and messages. Despite spending most of my life wondering where God was, I discovered that it is possible to truly feel the presence of the Divine.

Communicating with Spirit

"And those who were seen dancing were thought to
be insane by those who could not hear the music."
-Nietzsche

After my awakening, my intuitive abilities began to open up and on occasion I would feel the presence of someone's departed loved one nearby. I was freaked out beyond belief. I hadn't developed these abilities, so messages coming through were not fully understood but it was very clear to me that I was sensing spirits. My orthodox Jewish upbringing together with my cynical attitude to anything that can't be proved by science left me speechless. I didn't know what to do with it. I was extremely resistant and would try to ignore, deny, and dismiss these incidences. I didn't want it to be happening. I wanted to go back to a simple, normal life. However, I knew my old simple, normal life was one of depression and wanting to die. So, I slowly had to try and embrace all these crazy, weird and wonderful things that were happening to me, despite feeling abnormal and fearful. I had never been exposed to these things. I began to create new beliefs for myself that these things were real and ok. And to stop resisting what was evidently part of my path.

Michele, the lady whom I saw for meditation and had changed my life, does something else - channeling. When I first met her, she mentioned that she connects to her spirit guides and angels. I immediately said "whoa, whoa, hang on!" and literally covered my ears. I had come to her for meditation and was now freaked out. I barely believed in that stuff and thought it wasn't allowed within Judaism. I asked her to stick to the meditation stuff. It was only later that I relaxed about it and discovered that Kabbalists can do all this weird and wonderful stuff too. It has just been kept very secret. Well from me at least.

I read several books about therapists who managed to take people under hypnosis back to past lives. I then also began to expose myself to books and videos that people had channeled from the spiritual realm. Everything I read and heard resonated with me. It felt like this was the real truth and was coming from that part of the world, beyond the veil that we can't perceive.

I became less cynical about channeling. I realised that so much wisdom has been channelled in various forms. I even began to do it myself a bit, too. The veil has thinned between the realms and channeling is easier than ever before. It seems that the Divine realm is revealing itself more and more as the world undergoes enormous change.

Dreams: Messages from Beyond

*"We have forgotten the age-old fact that God
speaks chiefly through dreams and visions."*
-Carl Jung

I never paid much attention to dreams in general, nor did I think much about my own dreams and what they meant. However soon after my awakening it became clear to me that dreams have a significant spiritual purpose. I began to dream more often, more vividly and remembered my dreams more frequently. I often woke up suddenly, in the middle of a dream with a clear recollection of my dream and even sometimes instinctively understood its meaning.

One night, I dreamt of someone I knew who had passed away and it was clear to me that he was coming to me with a message. The dream related to an incident that had happened before his passing and I woke up knowing and understanding that the incident had happened in order for me to receive the message. It was then that I realised that those who have departed can come and visit us in our dreams. It was also this dream which gave me the realisation that there is a spiritual realm aware of everything happening in the past, present and future. And that it is from this realm, that we can receive guidance and messages.

As I mentioned in a previous chapter, after a frightening nightmare, I attended a dream analysis workshop where we discussed how our dreams are messages to us from our subconscious. It all made sense. These messages from our subconscious are messages from the spiritual realm. I don't know exactly who or what they are from, but they are clearly from our soul/higher self/guides/angels or departed loved ones in the Divine realm helping to guide us on our spiritual path. Furthermore, sometimes inspiration comes through dreams, and other times dreams are prophetic.

As I learnt to try to analyse my dreams, I understood that dreams are leading us to the path of becoming whole. This is what Carl Jung called the Individuation Process, leading to our true Self. To me, this is similar to or part of the spiritual path to enlightenment, salvation or redemption as described in different religions. As I learned about the Jungian method of dream analysis, I saw how so much of it was helping us on our spiritual path. For example, analysing whether we are wearing a mask or being our authentic selves and recognising our shadows - the unconscious hidden, disowned and rejected parts of ourselves that we have suppressed which need bringing to the light.

Dream analysis all resonated so much with what I had been going through and working on already. The only subject that felt new to me was the anima/animus. This is related to the masculine and feminine parts within us. I discovered that this is also an important part of the spiritual path.

Masculine & Feminine Energies

"...humankind is masculine and feminine,
not just man or woman.
You can hardly say of your soul what sex it is."
- Carl Jung

So, I discovered that another major aspect of spirituality is the balancing of the masculine and feminine parts within us. This is not about gender or sexuality. It is about the Divine masculine and Divine feminine energies that both run through each person, irrespective of gender or sexuality.

Both energies are necessary to create a human being and should be balanced to help us feel truly happy and harmonious in life. One of the energies is usually dominant in each person - generally the masculine energy within males and the feminine energy within females. These energies are known within all spiritual traditions. For example, as Yin and Yang within the Chinese tradition and as either side of the Tree of Life within Kabbalah.

Divine masculine traits are strong, adventurous, survival-focused, analytical, competitive, assertive, logical, rational, loyal, firm, singular, determined, goal-driven, giving and objective. Divine feminine qualities are emotional, nurturing, intuitive, gentle, collaborative, creative, empathetic, receptive, flowing, passionate, healing, expressive, wise, flexible, and patient.

I began to become aware of my own tendencies and imbalances. These energies need to be balanced within the world itself as well as within each individual. We have been living in a patriarchal world for thousands of years, where this Earth has been led by a more masculine approach. Masculine and feminine energies have clearly not been balanced within the world. I discovered that at this time on a global level the energies are shifting and balancing and there is a rise of the Divine feminine and feminine consciousness.

PART 4

HINDSIGHTS & FORESIGHTS

With the Benefit of Hindsight

"Life can only be understood backwards;
but it must be lived forwards."
-Soren Kierkegaard

My spiritual awakening and subsequent journey opened my eyes to the extent that the world simply did not look the same. It has stripped away so much of what I had previously thought and believed about this world and my life.

Everyone is searching for the truth. Whether through science, religion, or spirituality we are all trying to understand this world we are in, why we are here and how to make the best of this life. I realise that everyone has their subjective truth depending on their life, their beliefs, their consciousness, and their perspective. My truths have changed a lot. Looking back in hindsight from my new perspective, I have insights and hindsights regarding many topics.

These hindsights, along with everything else in this book, are from my subjective perspective and experiences. Nevertheless, it is important for me to include them here.

Self-Esteem with Hindsight

"Be Yourself, Everybody else is taken."
-Oscar Wilde

I wrote briefly about self-esteem previously, but as the saying goes, Hindsight is 20/20. Allow me to recap a bit. Throughout my years of depression, I became aware that self-esteem was an important key to happiness. Things got so bad that I couldn't even contemplate working. Irrelevant of whether I was qualified for the job, even things I was totally overqualified for, I simply didn't have the self-esteem to sell myself or to talk about myself. I couldn't even put a post on Facebook. I wondered why anyone would want to hear what I had to say. A certain amount of self-esteem is needed to be able to let anyone read anything you have written. To feel worthy. And I didn't have it.

I parented, believing that the key to life was self-esteem. I desperately wanted my kids to have their own strong self-esteem and not to suffer the torturous life I was living. I needed to make sure they had enough to go out into the world and do whatever they wanted to do. Nothing else mattered.

I believed my kids would achieve self-esteem through being exceptionally good at something. By being smart or talented in a sport, hobby or subject. I ran around trying out every possible activity to find the one that they could excel at to give them confidence in themselves. I also wanted my kids to be normal, popular, to fit into the box. To do what everyone else did. Isn't that where they would be happiest, being similar to everyone else, not standing out, being one of the gang?

Self-esteem, however, does not come from talents, looks, success, achievements, intelligence nor abilities. It comes from within. Self-esteem arises from loving ourselves unconditionally first and foremost. Our relationship with ourselves is the most important determinant for how we live our lives. Self-love isn't a simple task. It requires self-care, self-compassion, practising gratitude, acceptance, forgiveness, recognising and reframing negative thoughts we have about ourselves, releasing limiting beliefs and more.

Self-esteem also comes from being true to ourselves. From tuning in and listening to our inner self, our intuition, our heart, our unique soul, and from following our Divine path in this world. Only then can we be truly happy with ourselves.

Society measures success by wealth, fame, achievement and looks. Being successful is thought to lead to self-esteem but sadly there are far too many examples of people who have all of those things yet suffer with low self-esteem and succumb to depression and suicide. I have come to realise that the way success is measured is faulty.

What others are doing and the ways they are behaving should not influence us. In this era of social media, we cannot help but constantly compare ourselves with others. But comparing ourselves to others is futile. We don't know what soul journey they are on and what their unique role in this world is. The only way to self-esteem is for each of us to tap into our individual authentic selves, and no one can do that for us.

With these realisations, my parenting approach changed radically. I no longer tried to guide my kids to fit into a box. I recognised that they are their own unique individual selves.

Unique souls. Only they know what they are here to do and what will make them happy. I want them to find their own way by listening to their heart, not their head, and not to others. And to avoid that negative second voice in their head that tries to rationalise everything and has a million reasons why not to do something. The voice that is filled with fear, 'shoulds' and 'musts'. I hope that instead they tune into their intuition, the voice in their head that is speaking *their* truth, that is trying to guide them on the path of *their* highest potential in this world.

I began to try to adopt a more 'conscious parenting' style to help our children be themselves, to truly know themselves and know what their path is in this world. That is, to help them follow the things they are passionate about, not just good at, or what others want for them. The greatest gift I now believe we can give our kids is the strength, courage, and self-love to be exactly who their authentic self is. This is what leads to self-esteem. To remember that they don't need to conform to anyone or anything else, be it parents, family, peers, society, media, or culture. To trust themselves and listen to their heart, their soul.

Self-esteem will thrive only when we are listening to that inner voice, our soul, pulling us to do what we are meant to be doing with our life. That is, when we come into alignment with our true selves, not the influences, the conditioning, and the person everyone else expects or wants us to be. When we hide our true selves and avoid listening to what our heart is saying, when we fail to follow our passions and what makes our heart sing, we are not true to ourselves and we move further away from our Divine soul.

Anxiety with Hindsight

*"The key to success is for you to make a habit
throughout your life of doing the things you fear."*
-Vincent Van Gogh

My awakening caused my clinical anxiety to disappear. In the period immediately following my awakening my general anxiety disorder as well as several specific phobias, vanished. I still had the ability to be worried or stressed but a huge weight had been lifted and I tried to understand why. Why would my awakening cause my anxiety to disappear and what could this mean about the true causes of anxiety?

It was in fact only after the disappearance of my anxieties that I realised quite how bad they had previously been. Anxieties and fears like spiders, flying, heights, shopping, decision making, money, packing, a messy house, no longer sent me into an anxious frenzy like they used to. My kids totally noticed I was less stressed all the time. My daughter even commented that her mother had been replaced and upgraded!

In many situations, I recognised that the anxiety wasn't there when it would normally have been. It was a strange sensation, like I felt I should be getting stressed but wasn't. I wondered why situations weren't making me feel anxious like they did in the past. All the triggers to feel anxiety were there but I wasn't feeling the panic or physiological responses.

It was very evident to me that a big take away from my spiritual experience was how everything is exactly as it should be. That with only using our five senses we feel so separated from the Divine that we feel a need to try to control so much in our lives. This creates much fear and anxiety. With a higher perspective the fear disappears because our awareness expands to realise that so much of this world is beyond our control. Our extra senses are activated, and we have an underlying knowing that there is a bigger picture and a reason for everything. Things we consider negative or stressful don't have to be viewed that way with this expanded awareness - even without understanding why. Meditation expands one's consciousness and is well known to reduce anxiety and calm the mind.

I felt that anxiety had been trying to give me a message and get me on my correct path. It was trying to get me to surrender, to relinquish control, to realise that there is a bigger picture, to trust that there is a reason for everything and that there is so much beyond our control. It reminded me of the serenity prayer that is used in the 12 steps program for addiction.

God, grant me the serenity to accept the things I cannot change, courage to change the things I can, and wisdom to know the difference.

I have since understood that the 12 steps program for addiction are in fact spiritual principles. I have also recognised, along this journey, that many anxieties that we hold are from limiting core beliefs that have stuck with us from our conditioning or from past traumas. Fears that we have picked up from traumatic experiences or from our upbringing and culture.

Most humans are also not living fully in their bodies. We are spiritual beings in a physical body but many of us for various reasons are not fully grounded into our bodies. This creates much anxiety and much busyness in our thinking mind. Being grounded is a term also used in the psychology field and grounding techniques are well known to reduce anxiety. It became clear to me that I had spent much of my life ungrounded. I felt like I was floating and was barely here on the Earth: difficult to describe, but a feeling of detachment from everything going on around me. Being ungrounded was also a key player in my years of anxiety.

Depression with Hindsight

"Our mission on Earth is to recognize the void - inside and outside of us - and fill it."
- The Lubavitcher Rebbe, Rabbi
Menachem Mendel Schneerson

Before my awakening and subsequent process, despite years of therapy, I couldn't fully understand why I suffered so much with depression and anxiety. I put it down to my low self-esteem, perfectionism, and personality traits. After almost 20 years of depression I can now look back and see what I believe to be the numerous causes of my depression.

I had an inability to be true to myself. Having been influenced and conditioned by everything and everyone around me and by my upbringing - I had lost the ability and the strength to connect to my true essence, my soul and what it is here to do. I always believed we are here for a reason; I just never knew what reason. I never believed that diseases and illnesses were messages for us for how we are off the path, and for how we can change and improve. Challenges are here to help us, to fix our soul and elevate it. Bringing us closer to the Divine.

I believe that one aspect of depression is often our soul calling and pulling at us. It is telling us that we are off course and are not heading down the path we are meant to be on. When we are disconnected from our soul, we are disconnected from the God part of us. Deep down our souls know all the answers, why we are here, what we are here to do, experience and work on. When we are not following our heart, our intuition, and our passions we are disconnected from our soul.

Many of us have an unconscious desire for spirituality. We feel a void but have no idea that this is our soul pulling at us to align. So instead we try to fill the void with distractions, coping mechanisms and addictions like alcohol, screens, shopping, cosmetic procedures, drugs, exercise, work, food or studying. However, those aren't long term solutions. What we are really searching for is spirituality.

I also believe there was an existential aspect to my depression. Not understanding my calling in this world, and yet yearning to know what God wanted from me and the meaning and purpose of it all. This was a call for me to align with my authentic self and my role here.

I now realise that depression kept me stuck in a spiral of negative thinking, unmotivated to do any of the things that were good for me, to move me into a happier state and a higher vibration. The negative thinking created more negativity and caused me to believe and live in the experience of my negative thoughts. I was unable to love and accept myself and my depression and would avoid fully sitting with myself and my emotions to feel the pain. The cruelest thing about depression is it zaps the motivation for us to help ourselves. And unfortunately, it is only us who can improve our situation. No one else can do it for us.

Depression is asking us to tune in with ourselves. To find and speak our truth. Not to ignore our soul pulling at us. We spend all day long avoiding our pain, but we need to fully feel and process our emotions. They are here for us to feel them fully. And they are guiding us.

As I proceeded on my journey, other causes of my depression

became clear to me. Traumas from my subconscious began to surface to my conscious awareness, that needed healing and processing. These included repressed memories of traumatic experiences of which I had no recollection. It explained much of my depression, self-hatred, shame, and other issues.

With depression, one often ruminates about the past, wishing things had been different or having regrets. If there is something I truly felt during my expanded state of awareness, it was that life pans out exactly the way it is supposed to. There is nothing to regret. We cannot see the bigger picture, but we can trust that everything happens exactly the way it is meant to.

ADHD with Hindsight

*"Everybody is a genius. But if you judge a
fish by its ability to climb a tree, it will live
its whole life believing that it is stupid."*
- Anonymous

After the many changes following my awakening and the acknowledgment that illnesses had emotional and spiritual causes, I wondered about ADHD. I had a flashback to a memory, when eight years earlier, I had mentioned my child's ADHD diagnosis to a friend. "Oh yeah" she had said, "Indigo kid". I didn't know what she was talking about. I went home and googled it but what I read didn't make any sense to me at the time.

So, eight years later I went back and read about it again. This time it totally resonated with me and I was blown away.

Indigo children are souls who have incarnated here on Earth with a mission to help shift humanity into a new consciousness. They are here to challenge and shake up a lot of the old systems (like schools, government, parenting, etc) that aren't working. This is why Indigo (ADHD) kids are often strong-willed and defiant, they struggle to conform and often clash with authority. They are also extremely intuitive, don't tolerate lying, highly perceptive, creative, driven and change-makers.

They are souls with a specific role to play in this world

and with character traits to help them do so. Wow! And here we are medicating kids with ADHD to numb them and dumb them down to fit into our archaic school system. They are here to help the world evolve. They are born more evolved, more connected, knowing what we have forgotten, with spiritual understanding and wisdom.

Indigo children are souls born into this world to effect change. Rather than squeezing them into a mould that suits us as parents, the education system or society at large, perhaps we should allow ourselves to be guided by them to make changes and improve the world we live in.

Energy with Hindsight

"Surround yourself with only people
who are going to lift you higher."
-Oprah Winfrey

I t is only with hindsight and my new understanding of energy that I realise I was always sensitive to the energy going on around me. I now understand that I could often feel the energy in various environments and sometimes even found certain places drained me.

Most people are sensitive to energy to differing degrees and can sense vibrations. For example, entering a room where there has been an argument and being able to feel and sense the tension. Or sensing and reading that a person is suspicious. Or feeling the positive vibes at a concert or party.

I never liked crowded places, hospitals, airports, or supermarkets and now I understand why. Energies emitting from those places are stressful, anxious, busy, irritable, and fearful and it was, to me, palpable. Likewise, in those environments emitting positive vibrations. The energy in a room where hundreds or thousands of people are singing or dancing together is also tangible. And certain songs, especially spiritual ones, it's easy to feel and sense their energy.

We use the word 'vibes' all the time. Good vibes, bad vibes, positive vibes, negative vibes. Now I realise that it is about energy, the vibrational frequency that someone, something or someplace holds. It is the unseen energy in this world that we can sense and feel with our extrasensory perception.

Empath is a term used to describe people who are sensitive to energies. This is different to having empathy. It is the ability to sense energies and to feel and take on other people's energy and emotions.

I began wondering why we instantly click with some people and don't gel with others. Is there something unseen and energetic underlying everything? Perhaps it is the law of attraction at work, that we attract people and things which resonate with us on a similar vibrational frequency. It is often remarked that we end up similar to people around us.

I now understand why it is often said to surround ourselves with positive people. These people are vibrating at a higher frequency and being around them increases your vibration too. Most people who exude a positive energy are those who people love to be around. And then there are those holy or enlightened people who affect others just by being in their presence.

I also now realise why I suddenly had an ability to feel spirit and feel a closer connection with the spiritual realm. Everything is energy. Humans are denser energy and when we die, we still exist but vibrate at a higher frequency. Meditation expands our consciousness and raises our vibrational frequency. The spiritual realm and those beings in it are energy vibrating at a higher frequency than us humans. Therefore, as we raise our frequency, we are of a vibrational match to be able to connect to that realm.

The spiritual path involves the process of raising our vibration by clearing out the emotional (energetic) blockages that are residing in our energetic system and energy centres. As these are cleared and removed, we are able to lift ourselves into a higher frequency and allow more Divine energy to flow through us.

Keeping ourselves in a high vibration is key to spiritual growth and to being happy. Joy is a high frequency. All of the things science claims are good for health and wellbeing raise our vibration: exercise, healthy foods, meditation, practising kindness etc. Many practises within religion are also intended to raise our vibration. For example, gratitude is one of the highest vibrational frequencies. Expressing gratitude is a daily practice in most religions. Blessings are raising the vibrational frequency of someone or something. Blessing our food before we eat it raises its frequency. I had never thought much about energy beforehand, but since my awakening and discovery of spirituality, I understand science and religion in a totally new way. Recognising that our thoughts are energy with the ability to manifest by attracting a matching vibration seemed to explain so much. When looking at the world in terms of energy and vibration, and recognising that Divine life force energy flows into every living thing, I was seeing the world in a whole new light.

Religion with Hindsight

"God has no religion."
-Mahatma Gandhi

My spiritual awakening gave me experiential proof of the Divine. It also made me acknowledge that my understanding of God and religion had changed.

I became aware of how little God had been a part of my life despite living a life of tradition and observance. I now knew what it meant to connect to the Divine and felt a new understanding of the rituals of my religion from a spiritual perspective. I realised that my religion, the Bible, and its laws are a guidebook to spirituality, redemption and the Messianic era. If this is where we are aiming for (and most religions have a similar aim), then within Judaism, observance of the Torah laws was the suggested route. That is to say, by following these strict guidelines one can bring redemption. However, my new understanding was that this route is one of many paths to God. And perhaps the Judaism I had been living, of fear and condemnation, and a punishing and judging God was in fact incorrect. My awakening experience was that God is love, pure unconditional love.

In Judaism, the commandments can be divided into those concerning a person's behaviour with another person and those that involve a person's relationship with God. Regarding those between two people, I do believe there is a concept of reward and punishment, cause and effect, we reap what we sow, karma. I don't believe it is God who punishes us, rather that this world is designed so there are always consequences for our actions (both good and bad), in this lifetime or the next.

As far as the laws between us and God, I believe that they are here to teach us how to connect to God and elevate ourselves spiritually. Personally, I don't believe that there are consequences, punishments, or karma for not keeping them except for a lack of elevation. I wonder though, if, throughout the years, others like me haven't used these commandments to connect and elevate but rather to avoid Divine retribution and sometimes simply on autopilot. Doing them so they are done, box ticked. I believe this is a religion of fear and I came to reject that.

I now have my personal prayer and connection with the Divine. I realise that there is a constant communication with God, the Universe, through our thoughts, words, and actions and this is how the world works. Through our communication, prayer, intention and focus we are co-creating our own lives. I believe it is simply how the world was created. We create our own reality as we are made in the image of God and we, too, are creators.

I now believe the World to Come is in this world, that heaven and hell are here on Earth, and that heaven or redemption is a state of consciousness within this world. I believe that commandments regarding prayers and rituals are intended to help us elevate ourselves and that they do not involve punishment. And that there are many ways to pray and perform spiritual rituals and practices to help elevate ourselves spiritually and connect with the Divine.

My religious observance has changed since my awakening. I am more spiritual than before, more connected to the Divine and to following my soul's path. I can connect to my higher self, my soul, the God part of me in a way I never could before my awakening. However, I believe that religion at this time isn't a one size fits all. I used to live in a fear-based religion, fearing punishment, God, not reaching the next world etc. I believed everyone had to be religiously observant and keep the laws stringently as that was the only correct path.

The Judaism of my upbringing was an orthodoxy that had no real place for alternative practice, but I now believe there are many paths to guide us to where we are meant to be headed. And that once we align with our true self, our soul, we know exactly what route to follow. For one person that might be being ultra-orthodox and for another that might be not being traditionally observant at all. The important thing is spirituality and to tune in with one's own soul, the part of God within us.

Since my awakening, I actually find it harder to use the word God. God to me implies some separate being, a man in the sky. I believe God is the creator, the source of all energy, consciousness itself, of which we are all part, and exists within us. Not separate from us. I now prefer to speak of the Divine. The Divine implies God plus everything else emanating from God within the spiritual realm. When we have a spiritual experience, it is all coming from the Divine - whether it be God, angels etc., as everything is connected and all part of the One.

Life & Materialism with Hindsight

"Man's pursuit of physical desires and earthly possessions
is an indication of his lack of conviction that the purpose
of his existence is the attainment of spirituality."
-Rabbi Dr. Abraham J. Twerski

I had always been quite morbid. My friends despaired of it. Especially because I suffered from depression. It is probably quite worrying hearing your depressed friend talking about death and clearly not afraid of dying. Maybe I just innately knew the truth, like we all do subconsciously, that life doesn't end. The physical body dies but our souls continue forever. I had felt it so clearly during my awakening and at that moment the idea of anyone dying didn't faze me. It felt totally ok. I believe that often as one gets very near the end of one's life, one's consciousness expands removing the fear and anxiety that one might otherwise feel about death and dying.

I often wondered what I and others will think and feel on our deathbed. I guess that is what made my depression so difficult. I knew I wasn't living the life I was intended to lead. I didn't know how to. I was stuck in a rut. I knew that on my dying day I would be so disappointed that I hadn't been true to myself, that I hadn't done what I was here to do and been the person I was meant to be.

I love reading some of the wisdom and regrets caregivers for the terminally ill have collected over the years from dying patients. Things like wishing they would have lived a life more true to themselves, not the life others expected of them, wishing they hadn't worked so hard, wishing they had had the courage to express their feelings, wishing they hadn't worried so much and wishing they had let themselves be happier. Every time I used to read these regrets it would confirm to me that I was not being true to myself. I was not living my truth, not doing what God wanted me to be doing, nor what my soul was here to do and not living the life I was meant to lead. This is because when you are living it, you know it. So, I've learnt to follow my intuition and do what makes my heart sing because then I know I am on the right path.

Money is useful but it is not why we are here in this world and it is sometimes our obsession with it that can impede us from getting closer to our true goal. Nowadays, money has often become our focus in life. Wealth is often equated with success and happiness. Is that why we are here? Or do we distract ourselves with material desires and maybe addictions when what we really desire is spirituality? That was certainly the case for me.

It is very difficult to avoid attachment to the material world and to our physical body. However, life isn't about this material world. We leave it all behind when we die, including our body. What makes us us, isn't our possessions, our looks or our financial success. It is something much deeper, beyond the physical and the ego. It is our eternal soul that is who we truly are. Staying in the place of the soul rather than the ego helps us align with who we are and why we are here.

Meditation with Hindsight

*"Prayer is when you talk to God, Meditation
is when you listen to God."*
-Unknown

Yes, I am going there again. But that should tell you how important I feel it is. There are several things I have learnt about meditation with hindsight. I have come far from my beliefs that meditation is something only for Eastern religions or as a desperate last measure for chronic illness that people turn to when they have tried everything else.

I believe this generation is the furthest ever from spirituality. We are also the furthest ever from sitting still. We are human *do*ings rather than *be*ings. Constantly running, busy, tapping, flicking, surfing etc. Doing, doing, doing. We have no idea how to just be.

Depression, anxiety, and addictions are at a peak. The people who turn to meditation are often those who feel they really need it. However, I personally believe we can all benefit from meditating. Once trying it, we often discover it is really difficult, especially for those of us who can't seem to sit still with our bodies, let alone with our minds. Hence many do not stick to a consistent, regular practice.

I discovered that meditation is what prayer could or should be. It is what it was thousands of years ago. Through meditation, we can get to what we are hoping to get to through prayer: we can access a closeness to the Divine and receive guidance.

I feel like I turned to meditation out of desperation and came out finding God. Thousands of scientific studies have researched and documented the many and varied benefits of meditation. I can't quite express how key I believe meditation is to this world becoming a better place, to each person finding meaning in their life, fulfilling their soul's path, to bringing global and personal peace and redemption, and to connection with God, the Divine, a higher power. As the Dalai Lama said, "If every 8-year-old in the world is taught meditation, we will eliminate violence from the world within one generation." I truly agree.

I now realise that meditation is this phenomenal tool we have been given to benefit us mentally, physically, and spiritually. I believe that meditation is what had been missing from prayer for me and that meditating before praying or using meditation as a prayer with an intention is a whole other spiritual experience that many people cannot attain with traditional prayer alone.

I found meditation incredibly difficult for a long time. Some people love it from day one. However, it takes consistency, discipline, and persistence to see results. Meditation is not meant to be easy. Do we really expect connecting to the Divine to be easy? To happen on our first try? It makes sense that it takes commitment!

I used to think that our thoughts were private and irrelevant in our lives. I now realise they are probably one of the most powerful tools that exist. Our thoughts go out into the spiritual realm, are heard, and can be answered. Our thoughts have the power to determine much in our lives. It takes much effort and discipline to work on one's thoughts, but it is well worth the effort. And meditation is the tool that enables us to step back and witness our thoughts in order to consciously work on them. Many practices including Life Coaching, Cognitive Behavioural Therapy and Neuro-Linguistic Programming are aware of the power of our thoughts in creating our life.

I have also discovered that meditation is a metaphor for life. When we sit down to meditate and get distracted by itches, aches, emotions, and thoughts, we are not meant to avoid them, nor resist them, nor suppress them. We are meant to accept them, observe them, breathe into them, and know that they will pass. In life, fighting and resisting emotional or physical pain, only serves to make it feel stronger and increases our anxiety related to it. What we resist, persists. We should surrender to it. Like in childbirth. Give in to a higher power. Know that not everything is in our control. Life is always going to be full of pain and challenges. But when we push through the pain, through our comfort zone, and let go of the fear, that is when we have a breakthrough. That is when we heal, evolve, and grow.

I discovered that meditation connects us to our intuition, our guidance. Once we can fully follow our intuition, we are truly on our path of our highest potential in this world. Meditation is the tool to help us step away from our ego and embrace our soul. It can lead to real life miracles - yes, even in this day and age.

So Where Are We Now?

"If you want to awaken all of humanity, then awaken all of yourself, if you want to eliminate the suffering in the world, then eliminate all that is negative in yourself. Truly, the greatest gift you have to give is that of your own self-transformation."
-Laozi

My realisation of what the Messianic era would feel like, that it isn't so far off, and that many people all over the world are having awakening experiences like mine, led me to wondering whether there is a major shift happening in the world. I did some digging, and my instincts were right. I now understand that we are in the midst of a huge shift in global consciousness.

Individuals are moving into a different state of consciousness and the world is globally shifting too. The Earth is shifting dimensions from what some call a 3D state of consciousness (3-dimensional reality) into a 5D state. Humans and the planet are evolving and ascending. The old paradigm is a fear and separation consciousness, where we are still not aware that we are all connected and that we are multidimensional. The new unity consciousness is all about love, compassion, and kindness. That is where we are heading.

The process both individually and globally involves purging what cannot exist in this new consciousness. Much of the darkness needs to come to the light in order to be released. It is pretty clear to see that the world has hit a crazy level of chaos, mayhem, hatred, disease etc. This isn't what was intended for the world, but we are now headed in the right direction.

People are desperately searching for meaning and for calm. We can't keep up with the world at this pace. It is time for spirituality. Time to connect to the higher realms. The Divine wants us to connect, expand our consciousness, ascend, and elevate our souls.

The beauty of it is that once we do the work on ourselves, it has an overflow effect onto others and onto the world. We elevate ourselves spiritually by raising our vibration and expanding our consciousness and it has a ripple effect shifting others, too. We must be here for ourselves first before we can be here for others.

When I look at children nowadays, newer souls that are here currently, I see that so many of them are more evolved than their parents' generation. These kids are here, already more awake, more connected, more in touch with their intuition, their higher self. So many of them are already more conscious, knowing that war isn't the answer, that we are destroying our planet, that we are using too much plastic, that eating animals isn't our default. They have so much to teach us and much to contribute to shifting humanity. It is these souls that are going to make radical changes on this Earth and enable it to become a better place. So many kids of the new consciousness inherently recognise that we have come so far from what was intended and are helping to go back to what God really wanted and how this world was created to evolve.

Science is catching up with spirituality. Science has and is continuing to make discoveries and understand what mystics have known for years. Hopefully, one day soon, science, religion and spirituality will all merge into one unifying body of wisdom. At the end of the day, everyone wants the same thing, to understand what this world is about, what we are here to do and how to do it best.

The End Goal

"I think everybody should be nice to everybody."
-Andy Warhol

I had always wondered about the meaning and purpose of life and what I was here for. I would sing and pray for the Messiah and Messianic era, but it was an intangible concept into which I didn't put much thought. And I didn't think there was much I could contribute to it happening. My awakening gave me an idea of what that could look like and how it is attainable. An era where everyone is living in a different state of consciousness, in bliss and harmony, in a world of peace and love. Unreal right? It may seem daft or unrealistic with the current state of this world, but I truly believe that is the plan for those aboard the mission.

Achieving that state of consciousness is individual work. Redemption isn't something that is going to just happen instantaneously. The awareness that we have many lifetimes also helps this realisation, knowing that we are working towards the goal even if we don't achieve it in this lifetime. Our soul comes back more evolved and continues the task at hand. And this goal isn't just for ourselves. It is for all of humanity and the world.

Although the Divine controls and guides much of what happens in this world, we still have an element of free will. Our thoughts, speech and actions are our free will and can be used in a positive or negative way. The ideal is to be like the Divine, even whilst in human form: to transcend our ego, be kind, compassionate, loving, non-judgmental creators, all-knowing and understanding. The aim is to evolve and elevate our souls to the level where we can achieve all this and experience absolute, full pleasure. A state of enlightenment.

We come into this human body forgetting who we really are - a spark of the Divine. Our aim is to truly remember it and feel it, to be like God, connect to God, and to return to God. Connecting to the Divine, and magical, mystical, miraculous abilities, that is our birthright. It is not just for holy Masters, Sages, and Gurus. But it is something we must work at to access. Through meditation we can enter those realms. We can experience the Divine in our everyday life and detect the unseen hand guiding us.

There are many terms for this era we are heading into. Redemption, Salvation, Enlightenment, Liberation, Messianic era, Age of Aquarius, New Earth and End of Days. It has been prophesied in most religions. In Judaism, it was said that if the people didn't merit and succeed in bringing the Messianic era early, then it would happen anyway and begin before the Hebrew year 6000. If this is true, that means, as I write this in 2020, we have just over 200 years for humanity to raise its consciousness. I believe the process has started and a shift in global consciousness is underway.

My awakening experience and subsequent insights have led me to a vision of where I believe the world is heading:

A world where love, not fear, is the default.
Where violence and wars are eliminated because the overriding energy is one of love.
A world where external and internal peace prevails.

Where everyone has an overwhelming sense of Oneness, that we are all the same and all part of the One.

A world where there is kindness, care, and compassion, for everyone and everything, in every circumstance. For humans, animals, nature, and the environment.

Where spirituality overrides materialism and where we find fulfillment from within, not external means or material desires.

A world where everyone has what they need because there is plenty enough to be shared.

Where each person's masculine and feminine energies are balanced, as are those of the world.

A world where children are brought up by parents who allow them to grow and develop into their individual, unique being. Where each child knows they don't need to be or act like anyone else.

Where the educational system will be designed for the 'children of now'. A system enabling kids to find and develop their unique gifts and their soul's calling.

A world where people are healed holistically, recognising mind-body connections and spiritual causes. And where we have the knowledge and awareness that we can heal ourselves.

Where people are guided by their Divine souls not by their egos.

A world where the veil between the physical and spiritual realm is thinner than ever before, allowing people to feel the loving presence and guidance of the Divine.

A dream that I hope and pray we all will see realised.

Printed in the United States
By Bookmasters